CW00324191

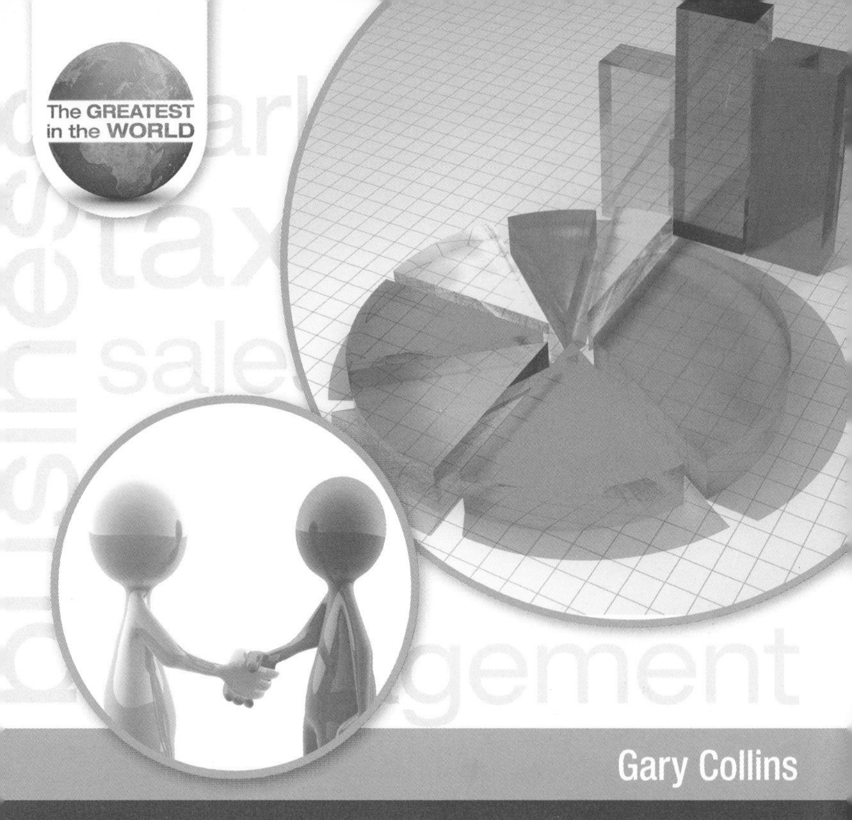

Gary Collins

The Greatest Sales Tips in the World

A 'The Greatest in the World' book

www.thegreatestintheworld.com

Cover images:
© Mikhail Tolstoy; © Cofko Cok
both courtesy of www.fotolia.com

Layout:
Shazia Saleemi
www.designspirit.co.uk

Copy editor:
Bronwyn Robertson
www.theartsva.com

Series creator/editor:
Steve Brookes

Published in 2008 by
The Greatest in the World Ltd, PO Box 3182,
Stratford-upon-Avon, Warwickshire CV37 7XW

A CIP catalogue record for this book is available from the British Library
ISBN 978-1-905151-40-0

Printed and bound in Italy by Printer Trento s.r.l.

For my father, Tony Collins, a lifelong salesman. Through a variety of products and markets my Dad has sold almost everything except ice to the Eskimos – and he could have done that had he wanted to!

Dad put me on the road to my sales career and was with me for my first ever sales call in 1975. Well when I say with me, he was actually sitting in a café just down the road as I wouldn't let him watch me 'perform'. It took me almost three hours but I did take an order – for about £30. Even in 1975 £30 wasn't much. But Dad was proud of me nonetheless and if it wasn't for him the next 25 years or so would have been very different and I wouldn't have had the opportunity to write this book.

Thank you for your guidance and support Dad, and the pride that I know you have in me and my chosen profession. I think of you often when I'm in a sales situation – you make me laugh and you inspire me.

It is the considered opinion of the author and publisher that the tips contained in this book are the greatest sales tips in the world and are written in good faith. Whilst the author himself has tried and achieved success with the advice given, neither he nor the publisher will accept any responsibility for any problems that might occur, or any damage or loss sustained due to the use of the information provided herein. This disclaimer has effect only to the extent permitted by English law.

Contents

A few words from Gary...

Thinking about what this book should contain made me think of the numerous books that I have read on sales techniques, most of which seem to have been written by academics who have never been in sales. Of course they can have a good idea about the theory of sales but I also think a long and successful experience in sales is more likely to make a book useful to the reader.

With that in mind I have written this to give you genuinely helpful and practical tips you can try immediately and see the benefit of in real terms – more orders and more sales. They are in simple categories so you can easily find what you need for any given circumstance. Sales can be broken down into a series of processes, and I will cover each one in order to help you find the steps and style that will suit you and which will help you succeed.

For the newcomer I can help you get into the sales process without forming bad habits, which can become difficult to change. And for the experienced sales person I aim to give enough tips and ideas that there will be something new, or will act as a reminder about something you have forgotten. It really is so easy for us to get into a rhythm in our techniques and not have the opportunity to review them, making any adjustments that would be productive. This book will help you revisit your own techniques and offer some new ones.

To be genuinely comprehensive this would need to be several volumes. Therefore I have attempted to cover issues that

I believe are fundamental to your successful sales career. So much in sales is about thinking a situation through and understanding the key issues. If you are unsure of how to handle a situation and the answer isn't here, use the experience of your colleagues. Never be afraid to ask for help and guidance – the only stupid question is the one that you don't ask...

One of my saddest discoveries in recent years is that Sales Managers rarely seem to coach and guide their sales teams. They give them targets and chastise them for not achieving those targets and for not doing their paperwork on time. But they rarely seem to do the most fundamental task I believe they are employed to do – be sales coaches to ensure every one of their sales team is operating at the very highest level of their ability. My aim is to become your 'virtual' Sales Manager who can coach and help you without being on your back for those damn call reports!

I hope that you will take this book with you so that, before you go into your sales call you can review your meeting objectives. Working in sales can be very rewarding. This book aims to help you in your productivity and success so that you can enjoy your sales career.

Have fun and smile – you look so much better when you smile!

The way to learn to do things is to do things. The way to learn a trade is to work at it. Success teaches how to succeed. Begin with the determination to succeed and the work is half done already.

Anon

In the beginning

chapter 1

In the beginning

There are some things that you should know—if you don't already—about your life in sales. The first thing I need to tell you is that this career is one that will only suit you if you are an optimist. You will spend many days alone and it can be very difficult day after day. Despite your contact with customers and 'the office' you are primarily alone in terms of motivation and handling difficult issues. It's YOU who has to decide whether to get out of bed in the morning and walk into that first sales call. It's YOU who decides which direction to steer your car as you drive away from your home and it's YOU who decides what your day's objectives are.

Communication is certainly so much easier and better now of course with excellent technology tools. However, you will have days when nothing seems to go right and there isn't someone sitting next to you to chat with or discuss last night's TV to get your mind off the difficult day that you're having. So you must be someone with optimism, drive and a real desire to succeed.

I'm certainly not saying that without these qualities you will not have a career in sales but I would doubt very much that it would be either enjoyable or successful. So if you are the sort of person who likes a challenge and has a competitive streak, welcome to your successful sales career – I hope it's a long one. And if you're not, maybe you should pick up the job pages and take a look at something else...

People like to buy, rather than be sold to

It's absolutely true to say that most people much prefer to buy something rather than feel that they have been sold to. You'll probably confirm this yourself if you think about your own experiences when you are looking to make a purchase. Do you like to walk into a shop and immediately have the helpful sales advisor spring onto you like a leech and try to sell you something; anything? Or do you prefer to look around and then ask for assistance as and when you feel you need some more information about the product or service? I suspect most people reading this will say the latter.

The customers or prospective customers who you go to see will be just the same. So your job is to help them make a good buying decision rather than try to sell to them. I'll talk later in the book about questioning techniques and it's by asking the right questions that you can find out what your customer wants and then help him or her make that good buying decision. Some call this Needs Satisfaction Selling and that makes perfect sense to me – find out what your prospect needs and then do all you can to satisfy it. They will then more than likely buy.

Do remember of course that we all do things our own way so because we know how WE like to buy that doesn't mean that you have found the secret to sales success – because we are all different. But by being aware of those differences you can discover the style and approach that will make you a member of the Successful Sales Club – rather than the 'also rans' who make up about 80% of the sales population...

Gift of the gab!

There is a widely held belief that the best sales people are those with the "gift of the gab". Well I can tell you categorically that it's a myth. The very best sales people are actually those who maybe I should describe as having "The edge of the ears!" In life generally, listening is a much underrated skill. Having and maybe more importantly demonstrating great listening skills is one of the biggest and most important attributes any good sales person will have. The reason that you will be successful in your sales career is because you will identify your customer's needs and find a way of satisfying them. How can you possibly find out what those needs are if you spend the whole sales call 'gabbing' rather than asking the right questions and then listening to the answers?

Early in my sales career, I spent about half an hour trying to 'sell' the benefits of my packaging product that I was responsible for. I can only assume that the buyer was having a slow and maybe dull day because he let me go on despite the fact that he eventually said no when I asked for the order. The reason he said no was simple – he didn't have any need whatsoever for any packaging products whether they were mine or anyone else's! Imagine how stupid I felt but I never did it again. It was a great lesson for me to learn and build on for the rest of my sales career.

Because you have two ears and one mouth the rule of thumb is simple – listen twice as much as you speak. You'll be amazed at what you can learn and how you can use that newfound knowledge to great effect.

Value is the King of Sales and the Queen of Service

Value should be the most important part of sales. That's what everyone will tell you and I think they are right. But how do you know what 'value' is to your prospect or customer, when it means different things to different people?

It can vary from the simplest issue around making buying easy to something more definable and tangible that the customer perceives as adding value to their process or company. So the first thing you need to do is find out what your prospect or customer defines as 'value'. Come right out and ask that question – then you'll know how to shape your proposition to meet that value.

Example of adding value

Some catering companies do no more than buy pre-packed sandwiches, cut them into smaller triangles and place them neatly on a plate adding a little garnish and a nice profit margin in the process. For the catering company this really does create value for money (VFM).

"Quality isn't something that can be argued into an article or promised into it. It must be put there. If it isn't put there, the finest sales talk in the world won't act as a substitute."

C.G. Campbell

Expectations

Most customers will expect certain added value elements to your offering. They are seen as a given because as time goes on we all want to increase our perceived value to our customers. That in itself will raise the bar as far as customer expectations are concerned.

A great example is service delivery. When I started in sales it was quite reasonable for a customer to assume that an order placed today would be delivered in around two weeks' time. To improve the perceived quality of service given to the market most companies worked hard to knock a day or two off this delivery time. Gradually it has reduced and now of course so many suppliers offer, and customers expect, next day delivery. In some industries the same day is not only expected but demanded. That's almost the rule to entry rather than an added value aspect to your offering.

That's how the Just in Time (JIT) approach to stock control was developed where not only do you have to specify the **day** that you deliver but also the **time** that you will deliver. So to give perceived value to your customers you have to find something that your competitors don't have the ability to give. But be careful and keep watching; they might not give it now but you can be sure that they will very soon. Then you have to find something new yourself as the bar is raised yet again.

Keep your eyes and ears open

As the person with responsibility for most customer contact you can be the eyes and ears of your company. It is partly your responsibility to identify what the needs of your target market are, not only now, but in the future. By understanding those needs you can plan to take advantage of the business opportunities that will be created for you and your company. Your feedback to your own organisation of those identified needs, will give you the opportunity to develop products and services to improve the offering you have over your competitors'. Many sales people under-estimate the impact and influence they can have in shaping the future proposition they will have the opportunity to present.

Who better to have that influence than the people who have regular first hand contact with the customers themselves and the key contacts within those companies? It's true to say that many sales organisations will have Marketing and Product Development departments which will engage in market research and customer/market profiling in order to understand the opportunities that exist and how best to exploit them. That doesn't preclude you from having your own very significant and relevant input. In fact because it is you who has the best working relationship with them, frequently your customers will be very willing and enthusiastic about talking to you regarding future needs and anticipated industry changes. These discussions give them a chance to talk about a subject that is naturally very important to them as well as influencing the future market and the way it operates.

Start the relationship building

These discussions, which are outside of today's 'business as usual', have the added benefit of helping to build your relationship with the individuals concerned. If these discussions eventually lead to new product or service trials this will undoubtedly cement your trading relationship, because you will be working together to find a solution for your customer and a new product opportunity for you and your own organisation.

Remember

- Be optimistic...
- Don't talk too much!
- Help your customer "buy" rather than "sell" to them...
- Offer differentiation (value-added) to your customers.
- Be the eyes and ears for your company.
- Identify both current and future needs of the market.
- Identify business opportunities.

It is our attitude at the beginning of a difficult undertaking which, more than anything else, will determine its successful outcome.

William James

Attitude

chapter 2

Attitude

I've met so many people over the years who have a huge amount of skill, ability and experience but they are not successful in what they do. Or at least not as successful as their inherent talent suggests they should be. This is not just about being in sales; it is relevant to any career path that you decide to take. And the reason for that lack of success is their attitude. I truly believe that having the right attitude makes the difference between being a winner or a loser. The fact that you are even reading this book suggests that you have the right attitude to learning and improving, which is obviously a great start.

Where better to look for examples of great attitude but to your sporting or celebrity heroes? Of course they must have that basic talent to succeed but many people have extreme talent – so what makes these people different? Why do they succeed when others fail? It's because they are determined; they are competitive; they take action and they make sure that they are successful in their chosen fields. There is a very old Chinese proverb that says "those who say they can and those who say they can't are invariably both proven to be right"... if that doesn't make immediate sense taken another look. My interpretation of that proverb is simple – if you think you can succeed you will; if you think you can't you won't. It really can be that simple.

Attitude makes the difference

Performance can be broken down into a simple formula:

P = **A** + **A**

(Performance = Ability + Attitude)

So not only do you need ability to be successful in your chosen field, you must also have the right attitude. You may even succeed without the level of ability that your colleagues have, but only if you have great attitude and belief in yourself and what you can achieve.

Always believe that you 'can' rather than you 'might not'.

You can if you want to

I'd like to give you a couple of great sporting examples of how someone's attitude can make the difference between ordinary performance and exceptional performance. And don't forget, these principles apply to you too – the chosen activity is merely a vehicle for someone's desire and determination to succeed. So many people talk themselves out of success before they start because they keep telling themselves (and sometimes those around them too) that they won't be able to do something. Maybe it's a safety net so that the expectations they and others have will not be so high that they might be disappointed. And that is a safe way to play it. Safe and modest and the likelihood of ever achieving something great is almost nil simply because those people don't go out there and try.

In my days as a Sales Manager I always knew which Sales Representatives would moan when I gave them their sales targets and those who would just get on with it. I also knew that the moaners were much less likely to achieve those numbers simply because they never believed that they could and that belief moulded their activity and therefore results. Think about the friends and colleagues that you have and how each of them has their own attitude to life and achievements.

Positive and negative

You can probably categorise them into positive or negative people. The chances are that the positive people are high achievers and conversely negative are low achievers. That is a generalisation of course and therefore not true of every situation but it's a pretty good rule of thumb.

Which do you want to be? I wonder how your friends and colleagues would classify you? Why not ask them and when they give you their answers ask them the reasons why – we rarely see ourselves as others do, so maybe this is your chance to get some good quality feedback which you can use to maximise your achievements. But be ready – you may hear something that surprises or even shocks you! But you need to know because if your friends see you as a negative person, the likelihood is that your customers will see you that way too.

The 4-minute mile

On 6 May 1954 Roger Bannister became the first man to run the mile in under four minutes. He actually ran the mile in 3 minutes 59.4 seconds. Apart from the fact that in doing so he broke the world record for the mile, Bannister's feat was even more remarkable when you look at the thinking of the era, especially amongst the medical profession. At that time it was believed that running that fast over that distance was physically impossible. The heart was thought unable to pump blood around the body fast enough to fuel the muscles to perform to that high level. Roger Bannister didn't believe them – he believed that he could run that fast and so it proved. I think this is a perfect example of how your attitude to a task can have such a demonstrable impact on the outcome.

Maybe what supports my thinking even more is that it's not a surprise to learn that having spent over 2000 years not running that fast because we didn't believe that human beings could, it took just 46 days for another athlete to not only break the 4 minute mile but Roger Bannister's newly set record. John Landy of Australia ran the mile in 3 minutes 58.0 seconds. So once it was believed and even accepted that it was possible, others achieved the same feat. And today the mile has been completed in less than four minutes over 4500 times by almost 1000 athletes with the current record set by El Guerrouj in 1999 at 3 minutes 43.3 seconds. I wonder if anyone will ever have the belief that El Guerrouj's record will one day be broken... it won't be by me but I do believe someone will!

Almost unbelievable

You may even think that I have embellished this story as you read on; I haven't. The man in question is called Cliff Young who was an Australian sheep farmer. In the early eighties he ran a 2000 acre sheep farm with his 81-year-old mother. They had 2000 sheep but could not afford a vehicle to get around the farm to round up the sheep when the storms came in. So Cliff Young would run around his 2000 acres to herd the sheep and bring them in. Now that's not the remarkable bit.

In 1981 when Cliff was 63 he decided to enter the Sydney to Melbourne Ultra Marathon. I'm not quite sure why anyone would want to run an ordinary Marathon let alone an Ultra Marathon! Just in case you don't know, this Ultra Marathon was 544 miles long. Can you imagine running for 544 miles across Australia? I can't.

Cliff Young turned up at the start to collect his race number and was greeted with disbelief when he told the stewards that he was there to compete. The thing is, there's more to this remarkable story that first meets the eye. Whilst the other highly toned athletes had the very latest equipment – Lycra running clothes, bespoke running shoes etc., Cliff turned up in overalls and galoshes!

The other thing that all the other athletes had was a support vehicle. A camper van where they could rest; because the known wisdom of Ultra Marathons was that you ran for 18 hours and slept for 6 hours. Cliff didn't have a van. Or anywhere else that he could rest.

The race started and the other athletes soon began to lose Cliff as he scuffled along losing ground. He didn't have the best of knees so instead of striding out like Michael Johnson, he kind of scuffed along, with just short strides and not bending his knees much. The main group was well ahead of him by the time nightfall came and they stopped for their sleep and recuperation. Cliff Young didn't realise that you were supposed to stop to rest... so he didn't; he just kept on running through the night! This went on for 4 days and 4 nights. He just kept on running! During the 5th night he caught up with the other athletes and overtook them and won the race, breaking the previous record by 9 hours! He later explained that as he was running he imagined chasing sheep as the storm rolled in off the mountains.

The point is that his superhuman feat was achieved because his attitude was one of self-belief. He believed that he could run for over 5 days and nights without stopping to rest. And so he did. Just think how powerful that attitude could be in other areas of life – and specifically in your sales career. Every single very successful sales person that I have ever had the pleasure to work with has had a similar attitude, that no matter how tough their targets were, they believed they could achieve them, and of course they invariably did.

Remember

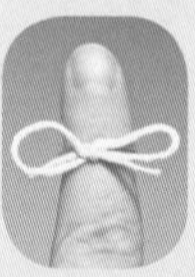

- Attitude makes all the difference.
- Set yourself achievement goals.
- Aim high.
- Don't accept mediocrity.
- Keep a very positive attitude – even when things go wrong.
- Be inspired by others – remember Cliff Young.
- Don't let others talk you down.
- Set new levels of achievement.
- Be creative.
- Choose to be happy.
- Being more positive creates more energy.
- Show the world that you are confident.
- Always believe that you CAN achieve your goals.
- EXPECT to be successful.

“For every sale you miss because you’re too enthusiastic, you will miss a hundred because you’re not enthusiastic enough.”

Zig Zigar

“The single biggest problem in communication is the illusion that it has taken place.”

George Bernard Shaw

Communication

chapter 3

Communication

Body language and stuff

Communication with anyone is not just about words. In fact, words are the smallest part of your communication! Various studies have come up with the general consensus that only 7% of effective communication is about the **WORDS** that you use. They have to be delivered in the right **TONE** (36%) and with the right **BODY LANGUAGE** (57%). At some point I'm sure you've said something to a small child or animal using a very friendly tone but with less pleasant words! Or maybe that's just me... Oh, how we laugh when the baby smiles at our words – but of course they aren't smiling at your words at all. They are smiling at your tone and your body language simply because they are more important.

The critical thing is to use a tone that is reflective of the message that you want to convey. This doesn't come naturally to all of us so it really is worth practising. And practice is a really significant issue. Many of us don't put as much effort and time into practising important issues as we should. Because we tend to communicate with each other with such ease we assume that we are good at it. Unfortunately that's not necessarily the case. Think about some of the people who communicate with you regularly – are they all good at it? So be prepared to put some time aside to practise the delivery of every element of your communication.

Drive time

Most people in sales have such a great opportunity to practise as they spend so much time in the car travelling from customer to customer. Rather than listen to the radio why not take this time to say your lines out loud? What messages do you want to give? What information do you want to find out? What benefits do you want to present? Say the answers to these (and other) questions out loud as you drive and try different tones that you feel would serve your communication best.

Practice makes perfect

In fact, at your next Sales Meeting why not suggest to your Sales Manager and colleagues that you spend some time discussing communication? Try out different tones and body language for differing situations and see just what an impact it makes on the message delivery. Do some role-plays so that not only can you practise but also gain feedback to help you perfect your style. As an example, try a role play with two people – person one is telling person two all about their family and hobbies and other interests, things that matter to them. Person two spends the time doing everything possible apart from seeming interested! They look around, fidget in their chair and general appear totally disinterested. Person one will find it very difficult to continue because the other person's body language is not suggesting that the conversation is interesting and therefore valuable. I find that it's useful in any role-play to have a third person involved who acts purely as an observer, taking notes and giving feedback after the exercise is complete.

Words don't come easy

I talked earlier about how important it is to get the right tone and body language, as well as the words we want to use. We tend to give the most thought to exactly which words will tell the story we want our customers to hear. Don't make the mistake of using statements that you don't feel comfortable in delivering. If it doesn't flow smoothly your customer will not be convinced that your proposition is the right one. Take the basic principles of the message and create statements that suit your own style and delivery. And practise. This is no different from being an actor. You are delivering some important communication that you want someone else to hear and believe. Practise alone or with a colleague or friend until you deliver your 'lines' in a smooth and confident manner.

Use technology to help

Although most of us don't like to see ourselves on film it really is a very effective tool to review our performance. These days of incredibly clever technology mean that almost everyone has access to a video camera – even if it's the one on your mobile phone. And it's even better if you have access to a digital DVD recorder. As much as you might not enjoy being filmed while you practise it will enable you to see what your customer sees. That's the very best feedback you can get – see it, believe what you see and make sure it's what you want it to be. And if it's not, then change it. Once you have done this a few times you will soon get used to the presence of a camera and ignore it, knowing that it's going to give you some very valuable help in your quest to be a great communicator.

Body language

Body language is critical to effective communication and yet most of us don't give too much thought to our own. Well, think about it – if you are talking to someone who spends the whole time fidgeting or scratching their nose how much time do you spend listening to their words and how much are you thinking that you wish they would sit still?! If you are standing, adopt a position that is comfortable but alert – maybe feet slightly apart, legs and back straight and hands clasped either in front of you or behind your back. That of course will be largely determined by whether you are someone who likes to 'talk with their hands'. If you are, then obviously you have something natural to do with your hands – but don't overdo it. Listening to someone talk that closely resembles a windmill on a windy day is rather distracting! By all means gesticulate – in a controlled manner.

It's rude to point!

If you'll pardon the pun I need to point out one specific cardinal rule for those gesticulators amongst you. Don't, under any circumstances, point your finger at the other person while you are talking. It often surprises me how many people do point (I'm sure subconsciously) and they don't realise just how aggressive that can be. You are delivering a statement of some sort that you want the recipient to listen to with a great deal of attention. You are very likely to reduce that attention level if you are pointing. It's a very aggressive act and will naturally cause the other person to withdraw and you will lose some of

"Being a salesman and an actor are not that dissimilar. It is a good lesson in covering up your feelings. No one wants to buy from someone who looks depressed."

Dougray Scott

the impact of your message. This is definitely something worth practising as it becomes habit forming (both to point and not to point) so make sure you develop the right habit.

Maybe the thing to remember is that we are usually pointed at as children when we are being told off. By parent or teacher the resultant feeling is the same – wanting to back off and get away from the end of that pointing finger. That doesn't change as adults – being on the end of a 'point' is an uncomfortable place to be.

Are you sitting comfortably?

If you are sitting make sure you are comfortable before you start to talk and in a position that demonstrates that you are alert and attentive. Also make sure that it's a position that you can maintain for a reasonable period of time without fidgeting. One leg crossed over the other will present a relaxed but alert style which will not distract your customer from the very important words that you are about to deliver. This still gives you the ability to move backward and forward in your seat according to what is required during your meeting. By the way, leaning forward is a real demonstration of paying attention so if your customer or prospect is talking to you about something important and you want to demonstrate that you are paying attention just lean forward a little and make good eye contact.

Buying signals

Similarly, if during your presentation or pitch the prospect leans forward it's a real sign of interest in what you are saying – so they might be ready to buy. This is a good time to ask a question as part of a 'soft' close: "Do you feel that (what I have just described) would benefit your organisation?" You don't need me to tell you that if the answer is yes you are certainly on the right path to a sale. So why not go for the full close and ask "Shall I arrange that for you now?" It's not an aggressive close – merely asking your customer if he/she is ready to commit. It they are not then you can continue with your presentation – nothing has been lost. Of course if they say yes, you have brought your presentation to an end earlier than you may have planned which gives you a little more time in the day to get one more sales call in!

One more sales call

Even if you just work the numbers game, an extra productive sales call each day has got to deliver more sales; just look at your normal conversion rate of 'calls to sale' and work out how much more business you could generate by being more efficient in each sales call and therefore having one more face-to-face with a customer or prospect each day.

Find out more

I am not an expert on body language, more an interested bystander. What I do know is that it's more important in your role as a sales professional than you might realise. There are plenty of books out there about body language and communication. I've listed one at the end of this book that I think you might find useful. There are some really useful tips for you to bring into your day-to-day communication and I strongly suggest you invest a little in something that could bring you significant rewards and success. Talking books are a good way to learn because by the very nature of what we do we spend a disproportionate amount of time in our cars travelling our territories from customer to customer. While this is good thinking time for considering the next sales call, maybe at the beginning and end of each day you should commit to listening to some learning as you travel to and from home.

Watch your tone!

I have talked already about the importance of tone – now let's consider it in a little more detail. Think about the people you enjoy watching or listening to and consider their tone. Are they monotone in their delivery? It's unlikely, because otherwise you probably wouldn't enjoy listening to them. A varied tone which is reflective of the words being used or the point being made is far more interesting to listen to and take notice of. This is particularly significant when you are being assertive. A strong but controlled tone will ensure that your message is delivered clearly and confidently. A varied tone is comfortable to listen to as long as it matches what you are saying.

As before, try listening to your recorded voice and how it sounds when you vary your tone. Find the right tone for you and your message, and practise delivering it until it's natural and confident. And remember, even though you might feel a little silly making your tone change your audience won't think so. Just analyse someone on TV. For me it's Billy Connolly – when he speaks his voice is all over the place and his body language is well developed. When we watch him we don't think of that – we just enjoy his performance because he is entertaining to watch.

Learn from good examples

Every day you will be exposed to great examples of communication. Even poor exponents of communication are good to witness as they show you first hand how ineffective we can be when we don't communicate well. Decide to analyse just how people communicate with you in any given day and you can use that to learn a huge amount.

Let's start with e-mails. It may be that your first activity each day is to check your e-mails. Each sender will use their own style – some friendly and chatty while delivering their message and other business like and to the point. Which works best for you in terms of how you react to the message? Are you more likely to respond to one style than another? If you are aware of that you can also be aware of how others might receive your own written communication. Become skilled in using different styles to different people to ensure you get the best response from them.

When you are in the car and listening to the radio take note of the styles used by presenters, news readers and DJs and how effective you think they are. Some presenters are more popular than others of course because they have a style and manner that more people enjoy. The same applies to the TV you'll be watching tonight – whether it's fact or fiction you will have many people communicating with you via the television set you are watching. Take note of how they speak, the tone and body language they use and which are more easy and enjoyable to listen to than others.

And of course during the course of your working day you will receive communication from customers, colleagues, family and friends all of whom will use their own style – some effective and some not. By just taking a little time to consider which methods are, in your opinion, most effective you can use that information to practise making your own delivery effective and well received. The most important thing to remember is that if you want to be truly effective in your communication you should tailor your style to suit your audience – not the other way around.

Remember

- Be aware of your words, tone and body language.
- Make them appropriate for the message you are delivering.
- Tailor your style to your audience.
- Practise your lines.
- Listen to yourself to become self-aware.
- Use your travelling time to learn.
- Effective communication will improve your overall acheivements.

Pretend that every single person you meet has a sign around his or her neck that says, "Make me feel important". Not only will you succeed in sales, you will succeed in life.

Mary Kay Ash

Prospecting

chapter 4
Prospecting

Clearly you have to find out exactly **who** your potential customers are in your attempt to grow your business. You then have to decide **how** to approach them and **what** your proposition will be. This can be either difficult or easy depending on how you decide to approach it. I would not suggest that the whole area of prospecting is easy – your success however, will be largely determined by the amount of thought and effort you put into it.

The first thing that you should realise is that today's prospects are tomorrow's loyal customers. I know that for many of you this will seem completely obvious, but not every sales person seems to realise it. Without putting the right amount of effort and thought into your prospecting activity the likelihood is that your attempts to reach sales targets year after year will not be successful. Therefore your planning time needs to include activities for both new and existing customers.

The Americans have a saying that "strangers are just friends who you haven't met yet"... now I have to say that strikes me as sugary claptrap! BUT you can adopt that attitude when thinking about prospecting; they are customers who aren't buying from you – yet! The key thing is simply that if you don't make contact with them to enable you to present your proposition they will never be customers.

The numbers game – ratios

I mentioned the numbers game earlier. You need to know what your ratios are. The world in one way or another is affected by ratios.

The definition of ratio is "the relationship between two numbers or amounts expressed as a proportion." Source – Collins English Dictionary (what other dictionary could I use?!)

Most companies will have a set of financial ratios which enable them to judge their overall performance and consequently make informed decisions. As a sales professional you need to know several sets of ratios in order to maximise your success. These are likely to be:

- Average success rate of the performance of your product against your competition.
- Average number of telephone calls needed to gain an appointment.
- Average number of appointments needed to gain time to 'pitch'.
- Average number of pitches needed to take an order.
- Average value of new customer (this can vary hugely of course depending on your market and sector).

Planning your activity using these numbers will enable you to build in enough telephone calls and appointments to achieve your goals. Let's look at an example. On average, you might need to make five telephone calls to gain one prospect appointment. Your conversion rate of prospect calls to new customer might be one in four.

And your Sales Manager gives you a target of gaining 25 new customers in the given year. This is when your ratios kick in:

Achieving 25 new customers requires 100 prospect calls which require 500 prospect telephone calls. Taking an average year with 48 working weeks, you need to make 10 prospect telephone calls per week or 2 per day. Now you can plan it and make sure it happens.

When you break down activity into a daily task it puts it into perspective and although two prospect phone calls per day is fairly minimal in terms of effort, it will maximise your chances of success. If you don't, that chance of success is greatly reduced. So even though the numbers come out at a rather frightening level make sure that you work them out – you need to know what it's going to take to achieve your targets.

First steps

So how do you find out who those potential customers are? If you are fortunate your company may have a database with prospect lists which you can use. You may even be able to get someone else to qualify it for you – to cut out the companies that are no longer in existence or have moved premises etc. Even if you do have access to such a great tool you should also look to find your own new prospects. The important thing to realise is that there are many opportunities for you to find prospects, some of whom will turn into important and loyal customers.

Take a look around

Every day you have the opportunity to seek out more prospects. It starts when you leave your home and drive to your first meeting. There is no doubt that during that journey you will pass many prospect opportunities. Keep your eyes open for company premises, sign-written commercial vehicles and billboard advertisements for companies that might have a need for your product or service. While it's vital that you concentrate on driving safely that doesn't prevent you from noticing company names that you can remember and note down at a suitable moment.

Internet search engines make information gathering easy, so a name is often all you need. Local and commercial radio offers another good source of information.

Use your contacts

Your own customers are also a source of prospects. Do be careful who and how you ask because this could be a situation where their own competitors are a very sensitive subject for discussion for that customer. However there might well be other companies that your contact knows about which they feel would enjoy the benefits of your product or service, without being a threat to their own competitive position. If you have been effective enough to have already built very good relationships with that customer they may even make an introduction for you – and those are the very best types of prospects to have.

“If eighty percent of your sales come from twenty percent of all of your items, just carry those twenty percent.”

Stew Leonard

Who else can help?

The same is true of suppliers. Some sales organisations work closely with other supplier sales people. These are usually third party suppliers – distributors or wholesalers. If you are a sales person for those third party organisations, work your contacts. Those supplier sales representatives will have built their own relationships with people who could become your customers too. In the right circumstances that supplier may even be prepared to make a first hand introduction for you – walk you in to see their contact in a dual workout. These really are very powerful and valuable because someone the prospect trusts is introducing you into their organisation. That gives you immediate credibility and a customer who is listening to you and open to your proposition.

My most successful distributor relationship worked simply because the salesman concerned took me into all of his existing customers who may have had an application for my product (so I benefited) and I converted many of them to buy my product through his company (so he benefited). This type of working relationship can bring huge dividends as well as making the whole area of gaining new customers so much more enjoyable.

How to make contact

Now you have to decide how to approach them. As a simple rule of thumb I would say that you should never cold call – turning up at the premises without an appointment. Even if you have time on your hands and have found a prospect nearby, by all means drop in but only to get a few details from the receptionist about whom you should make contact with.

You might be lucky to get to see the right person but in these days of busy people and tight schedules it's very unlikely. So use that information gained and set aside time to telephone your prospects to make an appointment.

Phone appointments

As part of your planning activity you should be spending time making telephone appointments. When you make these prospect telephone calls your objective is no more than to gain their commitment to a meeting. Be careful not to get involved in selling over the phone. That can happen all too easily because you are very likely to be asked "Why should I give you my time for a meeting? What are you going to offer me?" This is where you have to be skilled in giving enough information to gain interest in a meeting but not enough for the contact to make a decision about your proposition on the spot.

What's my line?

My favoured approach has always been...

"We have many customers in similar markets who are enjoying great benefits from our products (or services). I'd like to ask you a few questions about your business so that I can decide which of our products will benefit you most".

The suggestion that their competitors are getting an advantage over them is too much to ignore. You may have to say what your offering is but I would suggest that you talk in general terms rather than specific. This gives you some flexibility to shape your proposition once you have found out more about the prospect.

The knockout punch

There is one exception to that rule (about talking generally rather than specifically) and that is simply when you have an absolute knockout USP (Unique Selling Point). What I mean here is that if your company has invented the solve-all product for a specific industry or sector then go right ahead and tell them that – how can they refuse to see you?

You have to remember that you are just one of a number of sales people approaching that prospect attempting to sell their wares. You have to make enough of an impact to make the prospect agree to see you, as opposed to your competitors. And remember that your competitors in the prospect's eyes are not just those other companies who offer similar products or services to you but also every single other sales person who is seeking to get time for a sales call. One buyer will usually have responsibility for a number of products or product groups and they can't see every single person from every single company. You are fighting for their valuable time and you will only get that by sparking some interest during your initial telephone contact.

The other real benefit of having that knock-out punch is that when you call to make a future appointment you will have already created an interest and desire to see you to discover what other excellent products or services you can offer your customer.

What time do you call this?!

One last thought – think about when to make that phone call. Is 9.00am on a Monday morning really the time when the recipient of your call is likely to be in the right mood to be open to your request for a meeting? I don't think so. Equally 4.45pm Friday will probably have the same response. But early on a Friday afternoon might catch someone in a receptive mood as they look forward to their weekend break.

I would suggest that you avoid earlier than 10.00am because that's when people are getting the day started, checking or sending e-mails and just generally waking up. Late morning/ early afternoon will often be a good time both physically and psychologically. And the very best tip I can give here is if you try at a specific time of day and fail, try another!

Cold calling – anonymously

If you decide that you will ignore my advice completely and cold call at some stage let me give you some small pieces of advice. When you walk in don't have anything on show with your company logo on, i.e. folder or presenter. If you do, the person you are about to talk to will actually be making a judgement on you before you have had the chance to say anything at all. They are very likely to have a perception of your company—whether it's accurate or not—and will therefore be making a decision about whether they want to hear what you have to say. When that happens your opening line becomes almost irrelevant because your prospect has already moved on mentally and won't be listening anyway.

Starter for ten

Assuming that you are still there and the prospect is still listening, you really do need a very strong opening. The subject that is closest to most people's hearts and therefore gains their attention is, of course, money. So if you can create an opening that describes how you can save that person money or improve their revenue or profit you have a very good chance of gaining their interest – at least enough to go into more details about what you have to offer. You have to be confident and slick at delivering those opening lines otherwise you won't gain enough interest so that the prospect is prepared to invest some valuable time in talking to you for a while longer.

Not all detectives are policemen

Take a good look around while you are waiting to see someone; there may be clues around the reception area or showroom that will give you a steer on how to position your opening statement. Who are the other suppliers? What do they make/sell? Does it give the impression of being an innovative company? Is quality likely to be a key factor for them? Are there award plaques or certificates hanging proudly on the walls? There are always clues if you look hard enough and can interpret what you see; so keep looking and make some notes to ensure you don't forget.

This is an opportunity to make good use of the time you are going to be losing as you wait for your meeting to begin, so use it productively rather than sitting reading the latest issue of *Corn Growers Monthly* that they so thoughtfully leave on the coffee table for you to enjoy!

And don't forget to have that knock-out opening statement ready to deliver very early on after you have introduced yourself. This needs to be something that will catch someone's attention instantly and make them want to find out more. I can't tell you exactly what that should be because I don't know your product – so use a USP to make an impact.

Sources of information

Talk to anyone and everyone that you can. Receptionists in particular are a great source of information. And surprisingly most of the people that those receptionists 'process' in any given day don't speak to them other than to give their name, company and point of contact. If you strike up a conversation with them you are likely to get some valuable information which you can use, either then or at a later date. And they will remember you for the next time you call, which can only be positive.

Ask some general questions about the company, its business sectors and customers. Try to find out if any of your competitors supply them or if they know other sales people from related suppliers who you may know yourself. They then become useful sources of information for you to make contact with at a later date. Just one word of advice: receptionists are often also responsible for fielding the phone calls the company receives too so be sensitive to that and don't try to keep them talking when the call lights are flashing. Say that you will wait while they answer that call and then resume your conversation.

Other people's eyes and ears

The same is true of security staff – they know everyone who goes in and out of that building so might be able to give you some useful information if they are approached in the right way. The simple rule is to be friendly and not interrogate them. If you ask your questions in a conversational style you are likely to get a good response and some useful information to help you in your quest to make this a new customer.

Remember

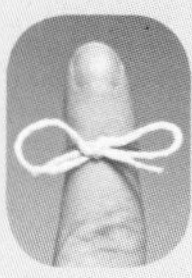

- Use your eyes and ears for new prospects.
- Don't "cold call".
- Use your existing customers and suppliers to gain prospect information.
- Telephone for enough appointments to reach your goals.
- Have a powerful "hook" to gain interest.
- Talk to as many people as possible to gain information.
- Don't sell over the phone.
- Practice what you will say to persuade your contact to meet you.
- Use a powerful USP if you have one.

Planning is bringing the future into the present so that you can do someting about it.

Alan Lakein

Planning

chapter 5

Planning

Get yourself ready

It might seem completely obvious that you should be prepared mentally before going in to your sales call. It's remarkable how few people get themselves into the right frame of mind as they approach that sales call. I talked earlier about a positive attitude and it really is so important that you are very positive as you approach the challenge ahead.

For some that's easy—they are naturally positive and enthusiastic people—but others might find it useful to have a trigger that does it for them. It might be a piece of music that you find rousing and makes the hairs on the back of your neck stand on end, in which case play it in the car. This will be particularly effective prior to a difficult sales call or negotiation.

What to use

It might just be a thought of a loved one or happy event. If a photograph of a partner or child brings a smile to your face then keep it with you and as a matter of course take a look at it before you leave your car to see your customer. This type of activity really can help to get you ready and prepared mentally for your meeting, making you much more likely to be smiling as you approach the office doors and start the meeting that could lead to a new piece of business.

When suits them?

Plan your visits. It is so easy to wander aimlessly from customer to customer without paying too much attention to the best time to see them. Some customers would prefer to see you at specific times of the day to fit in with their own routine – if you do that you immediately have them in a good mood, and conversely they are unlikely to give you're their complete attention if you are interrupting their routine. If they are relaxed about their own activity and time management they are much more likely to listen and be receptive to what you are telling them.

Know their routine

As you get to know your customer and build a relationship you will obviously know the best time to make your appointment, however, it's also very reasonable for you to ask that question when making the appointment with a new prospect. This is actually particularly important with a prospect because you are trying to make a very positive impression and by fitting in with the customer's working day you are much more likely to do just that.

The balance here is attempting to fit into your prospect or customer's day while also planning an efficient route to enable you to have a productive day. Giving alternatives often works and also means that, to a large extent, you have control of the situation by offering them a choice that fits nicely into your day's schedule.

"Sell a man a fish, he eats for a day, teach a man how to fish, you ruin a wonderful business opportunity."

Karl Marx

Route planning

How should you plan your route? What you shouldn't do is zigzag from one customer to another – criss-crossing across your territory and covering many more miles than you need to. Plan your route so that it flows in a nice efficient circle if possible, leading you back home to your front door! The M25 may not be the motorway of choice for most drivers but the concept of having that circular route is much more efficient than driving around the backstreets of suburbia to get your job done. It's a good idea to have a map of your territory with each customer 'pinned' to remind you of exactly where they are in relation to each other. This makes it much easier to plan your route effectively and efficiently.

Your journey plan should enable you some flexibility to cater for unforeseen events or demands as well as putting you in each piece of your geography on a very regular basis. If you need to have an amount of time each week or month in the office (or at home) to make appointments and complete administration, build that in too. Your Territory Journey Plan might look like this:

	Monday	Tuesday	Wednesday	Thursday	Friday
Week 1	Coventry	Nottingham	Rugby	Leicester	Planning
Week 2	Derby	Birmingham	Free	Banbury	Coventry
Week 3	Nottingham	Rugby	Planning	Leicester	Derby
Week 4	Birmingham	Free	Worcester	Sales Meeting	Banbury

You will see that there is a regular pattern for your area visits which means that it is easy for you to make your next meeting appointment while with your customer rather than having to phone nearer the time to arrange something important. The 'free' days give you the opportunity to fit something unexpected in at reasonably short notice or to use for that pro-active work you have been planning for quite some time.

Having a structured approach doesn't take away any flexibility that you might need. You can change things around but resist too much flexibility and change because that can easily lead to a totally ad hoc way of working which will reduce your efficiency and effectiveness.

Be in control

It is vital that you have control of what happens in your sales process. That starts with your time management and continues through planning and the actual sales call itself. During the time in the call when you are asking questions you are in control. Make sure that as much as is possible, you maintain that control throughout the call; including how much time you spend there. The most consistently successful salesman I ever worked with would always set himself a time limit for each call, based on the potential available. He would then ensure that he finished the meeting at the time he had previously decided. He kept control and ensured that he didn't waste time by being a bad leaver. (A bad leaver is simply someone who wants to get away from a situation but can't find the right way to do so). This allowed him to keep his sales call rate up and improve his productivity.

Planning sales calls

Once an appointment has been made complete your checklist for the call to ensure you are as organised as possible (see the form on page 149). I'm suggesting that you complete this form, outlining your objectives and important discussion topics as you make the appointment and therefore while things are fresh in your mind. A very good routine to introduce is each Friday afternoon to read your sales checklists for the following week to prepare yourself mentally for the coming week's activity.

Remember

- Consider what time of day suits the other person.
- Have a well thought out route plan.
- Build in some flexibility so you can respond to opportunities.
- Make sure you are a "good leaver".
- Maintain structure in your time management.
- Stay in control.

In your relationship
with others,
remember the
basic and crtitically
important rule; if you
want to be loved,
be lovable.

Anon

Building relationships

chapter 6
Building relationships

People really do buy from people. Of course you need the right product or service, however, it's also true to say that many good sales people hang on to business that their proposition alone gives them no right to have. The reason is simple: they have built a sufficiently trusting relationship with their customer that they are given a leeway when it comes to product or service performance or value. This really can't be underestimated and it should always be your goal to build such good relationships with your customers that they will find moving to a competitor extremely difficult. The opposite is therefore true – nobody will buy from you if they don't like you very much! It's just the same as any other relationship – the more you like each other, the more time you will want to spend with each other.

Unless you are in a market where you are only seeking short-term business relationships, avoid the temptation to take an order at your first or even second meeting. (If you are selling double-glazing I have a specific piece of advice for you – read a different book!) You are in this for the long term and you'll be surprised how relaxed you can make your customer feel by not being pushy; especially during those first one or two meetings.

It might even be a surprise when you end the meeting not having asked for an order; and that being the case he or she is much more likely to agree to meet you for a second time when you can progress the relationship further.

Make them trust you

Nobody will buy your product if they don't trust you. If a dodgy looking double-glazing salesman arrived on your doorstep, would you buy from him? It's the same whatever product you are selling to whatever customer – that customer must be able to trust you as well as the company that you represent. Then they are much more likely to trust your product or proposition. Don't attempt to skip this part of the sales process, because in many ways it's the most important part.

There are so many ways to build trust of course, and not being a pushy sales person is one of them. Think about what makes you trust someone. Maybe it's about people doing what they say they will do. Always. It's about demonstrating that you are truthful and discreet. Nothing will turn your customer against you quicker than you demonstrating that you cannot be trusted to keep sensitive or confidential information to yourself. Most people will tell others sensitive information at some time or other and they will normally expect that information to stay between the two of you.

Building confidence

Trust develops when people feel totally confident that the other person or company won't let them down. The integrity of the product, service and relationship is without question and there is a great feeling of mutual reward and success from the trading relationship that you have. This does of course take time to develop but it is also true to say that it can be developed quite quickly if you do the right things at the right times. And as I said before, doing what you say you are going to do is a great place to start. That's something that you can do on your first meeting and it's a good idea to create that situation so that you can demonstrate your ability to operate with complete integrity and trust.

Making an impression

Remember that you are making an impression and creating an image as soon as you pull up outside the company premises. Anyone looking out of their window when you park your car will make some sort of judgement immediately. It might be about the type of car you are driving (which, assuming you are employed, you are unlikely to have much control over) and it will certainly be about the condition of your car. Try it yourself – if two cars pulled up outside your house driven by sales representatives who you had invited to talk to you about home improvements which one would you have the best initial impression about; the one in the sparkling clean car or the one in the mud caked dirty one?

Make sure you are ready to greet your audience **before** you leave your car – don't walk up to the reception adjusting your tie or straightening your skirt. It's simply not professional. The advantage that you can use is that there does seem to be a real 'dressing down' among sales people in recent years so your ability to seem totally professional in comparison is much increased. Look professional, walk properly and talk politely – you have already started to build that relationship.

And do smile!

Looking the part

This relaxation in dress code means that there is a different expectation in the way you dress than there was some years ago. In the sixties it was deemed normal practice for sales men to wear white shirts (never grey or blue) and a trilby hat! Can you imagine that now? Of course not. So dress appropriately for your audience. Dressing down is much more common now but do beware – don't dress down TOO much. The days of dark suits, white shirts and dark ties may well be disappearing... BUT that doesn't mean you shouldn't be smart. Dress according to the environment that your customer sets.

Increasingly this dress code will be smart casual, especially in high tech or media organisations. But remember the first part of that description SMART. Clean and pressed chinos and a shirt can still look very business like as long as you are clean and smart – and don't forget to polish those shoes! Many people believe that you can tell a lot about someone by just checking whether or not they polish their shoes. It's about attitude and if you can't be bothered to polish your shoes regularly then maybe your attitude isn't what your company or customer is looking for. I am amazed at the number of people who buy shoes and then wear them until the holes appear, having never seen a tin of polish. That relatively small detail can spoil your outfit and image.

“It is not your customer’s job to remember you. It is your obligation and responsibility to make sure they don’t have the chance to forget you.”

Patricia Fripp

Classic look

I have to admit I still favour a suit and tie although I know an increasing number of men who wear a suit without a tie and still look smart. The most important part of this is that your customer should think you look appropriate. The same rule applies to women of course – look smart and appropriate. Apart from your customer thinking that you have made the effort it also makes you feel better. Let me share an anecdote with you...

Be yourself

Many years ago I employed a woman in sales. She had experience in Customer Service but not in field sales. She told me early on that she didn't want to make a big deal about her gender and wanted people to accept her for who she was. After a few months she called me to say she needed to talk with me urgently. She had started to question her decision and ability to do the job. In effect she had a crisis of confidence.

We talked it through and I explained that she should stop worrying about whether she was male or female and concentrate on feeling great herself. I told her to make sure that when she left home she felt as good as she possibly could in terms of the way she looked, whatever her style. I wanted her to go out with great confidence. Her performance improved almost instantly and the following full sales year she became the company's Top UK Sales Representative. She collected her award at the National Sales Conference amongst her peers and didn't look back. It was not all down to her appearance – however, the improvement in her self-confidence was brought on by her confidence in her appearance.

Don't be too familiar

Once you get to know your customer well there is a temptation to become over familiar or even flippant. Resist this trap because however well you get on, your customer won't want to be taken for granted – and that's how it will seem. Don't forget this is about building strong long-term relationships; your partner wouldn't expect to be taken for granted, nor should your customer. Regular reminders of the strength of your offering and the benefits that you are delivering will ensure that you are not being taken for granted as a supplier either. The strongest relationships are mutually rewarding and satisfying. Keep them fresh and enjoyable – and long.

Be sensitive to your customer

To a large extent you have to make a judgement here because different people will find differing levels of familiarity acceptable and even preferable. This is where your skills come in by understanding enough about the person that you are dealing with to know where to pitch your level of familiarity. This can become tricky when you have several important contacts within the same company. Don't allow yourself to behave inappropriately with one customer contact because of the relationship you have with another within that same organisation.

Let me entertain you!

Many companies disapprove of their employees being entertained these days and if this is company policy you need to respect that. If however, your customer is allowed to be entertained, find something different to do. Naturally enough it's great to take them to an event that is a favoured hobby or pastime, but maybe that's what everyone else does. Try to find something memorable. You can be sure who that customer will remember most... and if you are creative it doesn't have to take up your entire entertainment budget in one go.

It's a "man thing" – or is it?

Why is it that women don't get entertained as much as men? Probably because the traditional events are golf, football or other sporting occasions. But don't assume that women don't enjoy those things as much as men – they do! Consider other entertainment opportunities too such as the theatre and concerts, industry events, experiences such as driving at a circuit, hot air ballooning and spa treatments. The key is simply to give your customer something that is special for that person.

Let's spend some time together

Entertaining your customer doesn't just give you the opportunity to ensure you and your company will be remembered. It also gives you a large time window to get to know him or her and find out what really makes them tick – what their key motivators or critical issues are. Wherever possible arrange to collect your customer and travel to the venue together. Depending on what you are doing of course, you may get several hours travelling time to discuss all manner of things. You can yield more information on one entertainment trip than in several sales calls.

“If we are together nothing is impossible. If we are divided all will fail.”

Winston Churchill

Enjoy the day

The atmosphere is also conducive to having a more open conversation and often you will glean information that you would never be told in the work environment. But be careful – don't assume that the friendly environment you are in allows you to ask impertinent questions – they may cause offence. And of course your customer has come for an enjoyable day out so don't use it as too much of an interrogation session, however tempting that might be. You are there to cement relationships, thank your customer for their business and look forward to a mutually rewarding trading relationship in the future.

Customer relationship security

Having achieved the solid and trusting business relationship by going through the stages outlined in this chapter, how do you protect it? The answer has many elements to it, one of which is to keep on doing the things that you have done so far to get to this stage. Another critical element is to ensure that you make the number of people within each company (yours and the customer's) who have contact with each other as large as possible. (Refer to Chapter 13 – *Key Account Management* which goes into more detail.) Each of those people acts like a finger on the hands of the relationship, interlocking with each other to create the strength that you need. The more fingers that interlock, the stronger the bond.

Internal relationships

The whole business-to-business relationship tends to be thought of as one company having a connection with another; and of course that's true. For the sales team those relationships should go two ways – externally to the customer and the key contacts within that organisation, and internally to every department or function that can influence the offering being given to that customer. It's very easy for us to ignore that point and there will come a time when you will wish that you had better relationships with your colleagues; especially when a crisis develops and you need help to resolve it. Get them involved with your customer, take them on field visits, and make them feel involved. The list of people that you should consider building strong relationships with will vary from company to company depending on its structure and make up. Consider the following list – maybe you have these roles within your own organisation and could include them:

- Sales administration.
- Marketing.
- Customer service.
- Research and development.
- Technical service.
- Logistics.
- Stock control.
- Credit control.
- Training.
- I.T.

Remember

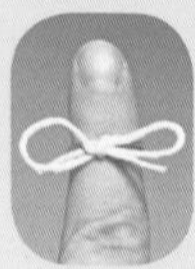

- People buy from people.
- Build trust.
- Create confidence in you and your company.
- Make a good impression.
- Be sensitive to the needs and style of your customer.
- Dress appropriately.
- Be yourself.
- Don't take your customer for granted.
- Use entertainment productively - be different
- Travel with your customer if possible.
- Build internal relationships.
- Use colleagues to secure the customer relationship.

Quality questions create a quality life. Successful people ask better questions, and as a result, they get better answers.

Anthony Robbins

Questioning techniques

chapter 7

Questioning techniques

Some basics

I have lost count of the number of times I have been working with a sales person and as soon as we get into the sales call they start to pitch. They get the niceties out of the way and then start firing benefit bullets at the customer or prospect. Now take into account that so far they know very little about who they are talking to or what that person or company's critical issues and drivers are and yet they go straight in with all of the reasons that they should take an order right here, right now. Quite frankly it's nonsense!

You must start the sales cycle by asking questions about the company that you are hoping will soon be a life long customer. What are their processes? Which products or services do they currently buy? Do they source them directly from the manufacturer or via a third party distributor? And so many more.

The answers to these and other questions will give you the basis on which you will build your proposition. So have ready a list of questions that you want to ask before you walk into the sales call and ask your contact if they mind if you ask some questions and make some notes – "That way I can determine exactly which of my products (or services) will suit you best and give you the maximum benefit."

I call this part of the sales call "blueprinting" because you are effectively drawing a blueprint of your customer in order for your own decision making to be effective in terms of shaping your proposition to maximise your chances of conversion (remember your ratios?).

Ask LOTS of questions!

The method that I have always used for questioning is to draw up a form for completion in front of the customer that details all of the important information that you will need. This is very easy to create with a document on your PC. By using this method you not only ensure that you don't forget to ask something but you can also create your own database of customer information by transferring your notes on to your PC later that day or week.

Who answers the question?

In my opinion the biggest sin you can commit when asking questions is to give the answer yourself (this applies to other situations and not just sales)! I have become increasingly irritated by interviewers on the radio and television who ask a question and then offer alternatives for the respondent to choose from! Maybe it is neither of those options but actually some people will choose one just to make it easy for them. "Why did you decide to move abroad? Was it because of the warmer weather over there or because you were just fed up with living in England?" The next time you see someone interviewed on TV take note of how the questions are asked. Interestingly the interviewer is actually using a closing technique (which is covered in Chapter 11 – *Closing the sale*).

So the solution is simple – ask a question… and then shut up! Even if there is silence for a while, don't feel obliged to fill the gap. This is merely thinking time and you will get your answer as long as you give the customer the opportunity to talk in their own words. If the situation is rather difficult, perhaps in a negotiation situation, that silence from you is incredibly powerful so it is even more important that you don't break it.

Get some feedback

This is not as simple as it seems for some people. They seem to feel compelled to offer their own answer so if this is you, practise just asking questions and then being totally quiet while you wait for the response. You may not realise that you do this so ask your family, friends and colleagues, not all of us are very self-aware and we tend to do things that we are unaware of. This is really important so take some time on it and practise. Very few sales skills courses I have witnessed take enough time covering questioning techniques and I believe that it's the foundation of all that follows.

When do I ask questions?

The simple answer is 'at every opportunity'. Questioning is not an activity that happens on the first or second sales calls only. Every time you are in a contact situation find some questions to ask. If you know the customer very well those questions might be very simple ones about the current activity within the organisation or market. There is always something that you don't know and it will prove very useful to you later to have the maximum amount of up to date knowledge possible about your customer and their market.

If you can't think of any specific questions to ask you can fall back on some basic ones like:

"How is the current economic climate affecting your market?"

"Which part of your manufacturing process is giving you the biggest headache right now?"

"Is there one thing that you would change within your manufacturing process if you could?"

"What things are causing you the greatest concerns at the moment?"

"How do you measure product (or service) performance?"

Needs satisfaction selling

Just think how pleased your customer would be if you could help make just one of those situations better with your own product or service. And of course that would lead not only to more business now and in the future but also increase your credibility and trust with that customer. More than one salesman has lost business because they stopped asking questions throughout the relationship and made incorrect assumptions about their customer's needs and therefore didn't continue to satisfy them.

Ask another question!

You can't have too much information but you can certainly have too little...

"If you don't sell, it's not the product that's wrong, it's you."

Estee Lauder

When you get information always try to find another question so you can delve a bit deeper into either that company or individual and the needs that each may have. So for example you may ask how a customer carries out a particular manufacturing process. Once you have been given the answer ask some 'why' or 'what' questions:

"Why do you do it that way?"

"Why did you decide to buy from that particular supplier?"

This will help you really understand the situation and more importantly the reasons behind the decisions that have already been made by that company at that time. As before, this will enable you to shape your own proposition to maximise the chances of success.

"Open" questions

In the early stages of a business relationship in particular you should ask open questions. These are questions which make the other person give you information rather than just answer yes or no. So for example ask how they currently make their world famous widget? Your customer will have to give you lots of useful information which may help you later in the sales call. Open questions will typically—but not always—start with 'how' or 'why'.

Try asking questions such as:

"Why did you decide to do it that way?"

"Who have you had success with previously?"

"What prompted you to make this enquiry?"

"What do you need this product/service to do?"

"What is the best way of making this happen?"

"What challenges does your current process create?"

"What are the best things about that process?"

"Closed" questions

Closed questions are those that (usually) only require one word answers like yes and no. They are still very useful but will not open up discussion in themselves. The best time to use closed questions is when you want to pin down something specific:

"Do you have any time restraints for making this happen?"

"Is anyone else is involved in this decision?"

"So if I understand you correctly, the fact that your current supplier can't deliver on Fridays is a real problem to you?"

What a great opportunity for you especially if you can deliver on Fridays. In that example you could respond with a huge benefit by simply stating that you can and will deliver on Fridays and "When would you like the first delivery to be made?"

In its own way this type of question is just as powerful as an information-gathering question – it simply offers different information and should be used at different times.

Listening skills

Now that you have managed to get your contact to talk to you about the important business issues it should be obvious that you must listen to the answers that are given. Most importantly, as well as listening you should also demonstrate that you are listening by using 'active listening' techniques. These are simply actions on your part, which convey your interest and understanding of what is being said. I think one of the reasons that many sales people don't listen as well as they should is because they are actually thinking about what they want to ask or say next. While that is important it's not useful if it means that your customer thinks that you are not listening to them. Why should they bother to answer your questions if you are not going to listen to what they say?

Take a note

One way of solving that problem is simply to use the blueprinting form that I mentioned earlier. If your next question is already written down you can concentrate fully on what is being said and actually engage in a dialogue rather than a question and answer session.

This is an important skill to have in all walks of life and it's sad to say that fewer people have it than I would hope – especially in a sales environment.

Active listening

There are some simple things that you can do to demonstrate these active listening skills. They can be as simple as making good eye contact and nodding your head at suitable intervals to show that you understand what is being said. Including an occasional yes or no also demonstrates your attention. This really does encourage people to talk to you and give you the information that you are seeking and which will prove useful to you further along the sales process.

A key action when listening is also to paraphrase what they have explained to you in such a way that it demonstrates to them that you have understood. They in turn will confirm the points made and both people then know that they understand each other.

Get the habit

This is certainly something that doesn't come naturally to many people and is worth practising at home or in a business environment. When you are talking to your friends and family or indeed your colleagues, use the simple techniques that I have described above until they become a habit. I have mentioned the importance of forming good habits before and I really can't emphasise that enough. There is no doubt that those people in any walk of life who have created good habits in what they do are invariably successful. The other way of looking at it is that successful people almost always have excellent habits in the way that they operate. Whichever way you view things it's clear that forming those good habits will lead you along a successful path.

Role-plays

This is another skill, which is easily practised using role-plays at sales meetings. Scripts can easily be written which can be played out for just 30 minutes on a regular basis between colleagues, which will lead to good practice when you are in front of your customers.

Don't forget what you've just been told

Make sure that you take notes when you are in your sales call, especially when asking a series of questions. I think it's a good idea (and good manners) to ask if the person you are speaking to minds if you make a few notes about what you are discussing. I have never been refused and it does demonstrate an element of respect for the other person. If you use an adaptation of your blueprinting form complete it as you go; it also acts as a prompt for your next question.

Mental gymnastics

You will need a certain amount of mental agility when writing notes and asking questions at the same time. I think it's a bit like driving a car – at first there seem to be too many things to think about and do, but you soon get the hang of it. And don't worry about allowing pauses to occur as you finish writing what you have just been told. Your customer won't expect you to have shorthand so will be happy to wait a few seconds as you finish taking the notes that will help you provide him with future benefits. As well as being efficient for you it also demonstrates that efficiency to your customer.

Be efficient

As part of your trust building you want your customer to know that you are someone who is on top of things; well-organised and effective in remembering important issues and future activities. If you promise to do something after the sales call has finished and your customer sees you write it down there will immediately be a confidence that you will do it. If you don't write it down the reverse could be true.

Create a positive perception

As you will have heard many people say before reading this book, perception is often more important than reality. That's certainly true in sales, as the confidence that you can create in the mind of your prospect or customer will strongly influence their desire and inclination to do business with you. By demonstrating your efficiency and commitment you will create that confidence and build a very positive perception of yourself and your company. The added benefit is simply that your own credibility will be easily transferred onto the proposition that you are presenting to your customer.

Summarise

Once you have gathered information through your questioning techniques and noted the relevant issues, it's a good idea to summarise to your customer what you intend to do with that information. Explain if for example, you are going to explore the best products, services or methods with your technical colleagues before returning with your recommendations. Once again this will instil confidence in your customer – as long as you do it of course!

You can also use this summary to remind the customer if he or she has committed to doing something for you to help develop the trading relationship.

Remember

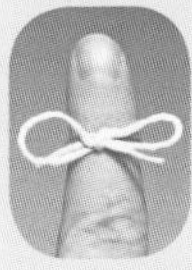

- Ask lots of questions.
- Have a supply of fall-back questions.
- Ask and then shut up and listen.
- Use both open and closed questions.
- Take notes.
- Be efficient.
- Create positive perceptions.
- Summarise actions.

“In selling as in medicine, prescription before diagnosis is malpractice.”

Tony Alesandra

Your proposal

chapter 8

Your proposal

If you are selling a product as opposed to a service let your customer see your product... take some samples with you and put it or them on the customer's desk as you start talking. Their natural curiosity will make it impossible for them not to pick it up and take a closer look! Being inquisitive is one of our human characteristics and you can use that to your advantage.

If you sell a service take something that they can look at instead; these might include photographs, glossy brochures or testimonials. As soon as they pick up the product or brochure they are showing interest (a potential buying signal) and you can start to talk positively about them owning and using it. It's almost time to go in for the order and because your prospect has shown interest it can be a gentle close.

As with most things in life this is about balance – take enough samples to gain interest but not so many that you merely create confusion. Invariably if you have ten versions of the same thing but maybe in different colours, the customer will find one to choose. But because you have given so much choice that decision becomes more difficult. If you offered four colours the chances are that they would still find something that they like and would make the choice more simply.

You want literature?

Don't leave literature! That's the oldest brush-off in the book. "Leave me some literature and I'll think about it". What he means is I'm not interested but I haven't got the bravery or good manners to tell you to your face! If the customer wants to think about your proposition, tell them it's a good idea and why don't you think about it together? That way you can help answer any questions that might be troubling them. Or at the very least you'll find out why they don't want to buy right now. It's an objection and leaving literature won't handle it.

Literature is a very powerful marketing and sales tool – but very few people buy anything from literature unless it's a shopping catalogue for the individual consumer, which is a very different situation. In commercial sales environments people do not buy from the literature that you have just left with them. They put it in their desk tray (if it makes it past the waste paper basket) where it's covered by the next piece of literature left by the next sales representative to call.

The exception to the rule

My view is that the only time that you should leave literature is after you have taken an order. By all means then leave them the information that will convince them that they have made a good buying decision. But don't fall into the trap of leaving literature in lieu of a more positive conversation.

Be an expert

Know your product. You may well have sales aids and literature but you really have to know your product well to deliver a successful sales pitch. When you are asked a question you will create lots more trust in you AND your product if you can answer straight away and with confidence. Practise with colleagues or family to make sure you could take this as your specialist subject on Mastermind! Just imagine how you would feel if the person answering a question you'd put to them started to stutter and hesitate – how confident would you be?

Back to school

Over time you will obviously become more competent at answering questions about your offering simply through experience. In your early days make sure that you practise and study to increase your knowledge and therefore your ability to be impressive. You can never know too much but you can know too little.

Since a rather famous television advert some years ago a new phrase has crept into the vocabulary of the average sales person: "I don't know but I know a man who does" or "I don't know but I'll find out and let you know". Now this isn't the worst thing you could say but it certainly doesn't instil confidence in your prospect or customer. So do everything that you can to know as much as you can – not just about the features of your product or service but also the benefits that you can bring that customer.

Practice makes perfect

Practise demonstrating. If your product is one that can be demonstrated make sure you are very good at doing so. Nothing will eliminate confidence in you and your product more than a poor or unsuccessful demonstration. Conversely, an impressive demonstration has a very good chance of sealing the deal. So make sure you practise over and over again before you attempt demonstrating it – especially with a new product. I liken this to a magician on stage. For that magician to be totally impressive he or she needs to be slick and skilful, if not you won't believe the magic. The same applies to your demonstrations so make sure that you are slick and skilful yourself.

In their own hands

Once you have carried out some form of demonstration you should look for opportunities for the customer to try the product themselves. This is particularly the case if you are selling a product used in a manufacturing process. Once you have shown the product in use yourself give it to the person who will be using it in the future. If that person likes what it does they will be a great advocate for you and you are almost home and dry.

All present and correct

The preparation that I spoke of earlier also applies to demonstration equipment and samples too of course. You should set aside some time each week—maybe last thing Friday—to make sure that your demonstration equipment is in good working order, clean and presentable, and that any consumables that you need are in good supply. It is

"No sale is really complete until the product is worn out, and the customer is satisfied."

L.L. Bean

unforgivable to arrive at your prospect without the appropriate samples or equipment to carry out a successful demonstration. And there is only one person who has control over that – you.

Be stylish

The style of your presentation is going to strongly influence whether or not you will make a successful bid. If you have thoroughly blueprinted previously you can tailor your content to match the needs and opportunities of your customer. The more closely you mirror their situation the more they will believe that you care about them and want to help them. We all like to be helped along the way at some point and this is a great start. And don't forget to use a style that suits the individual that you are talking to... a Managing Director and a shop floor worker will expect different things; both will influence your chances of success. Your ability to be a chameleon is directly linked to your likelihood of success.

Again preparation is key: know your audience and produce a proposition that will answer all the questions that might come to mind, as well as offering them the benefits and advantages that your product or service will give. Use appropriate vehicles of delivery whether it's a PowerPoint presentation to a Board or a series of statements to a shop floor operative. Have your own style by all means – if you can tailor that style to suit your audience so much the better.

Explain the benefits

Always sell benefits – not features. The fact that your product is blue probably doesn't matter to the customer. What is important is what your product will do for that customer or their business. If you can tangibly show that you can save money, improve efficiency or add value how can you fail to take an order? So by all means talk about features but it's the benefits that will make the customer want to buy from you.

Pencil selling

You may have heard of a 'Pencil Sell' which is simply where you produce on paper the information that supports your proposition. This can be incredibly powerful and it's worth the preparation before meeting your prospect. Always present the benefits of your product in the highest terms. So talk about annual savings rather than unit savings. Or annual profit gains rather than unit margins. Imagine yourself being presented with a proposition for a product that is 1p cheaper than the competition. It's not very impressive. But if I told you that I use 4,000,000 of that product each year the saving would be £40,000 – much more impressive, so that's what you talk about.

Sales tools

References and testimonials can be incredibly strong when trying to convince your customer to buy. You can take (at least) two approaches to this issue. Try to get testimonials from other companies that you know deal with your customer so their opinion is credible and trusted. It may be a product that is used in conjunction with yours and therefore complements it well.

You can also try using a testimonial from one of their competitors. If they think that their biggest rival has found a better supplier or method or cost they will be very keen not to be left behind. Play on that competitive nature...

The power of testimonials from credible companies cannot be over-stated; here is a current user of your product or service who is strongly placed in the sector saying what a great benefit they have enjoyed as a result of buying from you. When you say how good you are the customer may not believe you simply because you are bound to say that. When an independent and trusted company or person makes that same statement your credibility immediately gets a massive boost.

Remember

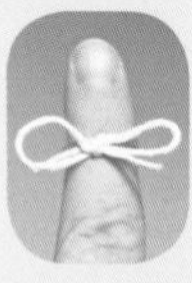

- Show and tell.
- Don't leave literature.
- Be an expert.
- Sell benefits not features.
- Personalise those benefits
- Use sales tools effectively.
- Practise demonstration techniques.
- Tailor your style to suit the audience.

> Exclusivity and uniqueness are most critical to wealth consumers. Having too many stores can take away from exclusivity.

Miton Pedraze

Unique selling points

chapter 9
Unique selling points

I talked earlier about Unique Selling Points (USPs) and how important they are. A USP is exactly what it says it is; something that you offer that your competitors can't; something that makes your proposition stand out from the crowd as being unique and beneficial. One of the reasons that marketing should identify them is that I would expect to see the USPs listed in any literature and packaging that is designed for product launches or introductions. It is so important to recognise the value these USPs give you when delivering your proposition to your prospect or customer, so you must know what they are and how they will benefit that company or person.

USPs need to be explained and understood to ensure the connection can be made between the USP and the direct benefits that apply to the use of the product or service. It is important that you present that connection to the person you are dealing with rather than assume it will be made. And also remember that benefits can be expressed in terms of benefits to the organisation OR the individual, or both. We might present products or services where perhaps the main benefit is time saving, which does benefit the company of course, but also shows great benefit to the people within that company. Knowing your Unique Selling Points is one of the most important weapons in your armoury and will make the convincing part of the sales process much easier.

How unique should they be?

Uniqueness means exactly that; there is no other. The reality is however, that the majority of sales people will not be fortunate enough to have a product with a true USP. So what then? The answer is simple – you have to create a statement about your product, service or company which is sufficiently strong and compelling that it is unique in its entirety. That uniqueness might be a combination of things that you are able to bring together in a way that your competitors can't. If you think about consumable products—maybe photocopying paper—assuming that the different weights of paper (gsm) are available from many sources, there doesn't seem to be much that's unique in that. If however, one company can bundle that with every other office consumable likely to be needed by any given customer, with an efficient on-line ordering system, electronic billing and Internet banking invoice settlement, that total package might be unique. And there is your USP.

If you don't have anything unique

If you are in that unfortunate position of not having any USPs for your product or service there is still hope for you. You need to find a way of minimising the significance of other USPs in the market or amongst your competitors and concentrate on the benefits of your offering. Even though it isn't unique it does still have benefits, even if the only benefit that you have is price. It is both more rewarding and more satisfying to be able sell on things other than price but some organisations do create their business plans and selling strategy around delivering the lowest market price.

They lose the ability to positively affect both revenue and profit lines by selling USPs (which by nature tend to command higher selling prices) so they create a strategy which delivers other company benefits through lowest like for like market pricing.

Internet example

A hugely successful example of this is Internet aggregator sites. These are the sites that you see advertised offering you just one click of your mouse to identify all of the best deals available online. For example, they might be flights – you type in where you want to go and when, and with that click of the mouse your screen is full of hundreds of companies offering you the latest deals on cheap flights to your chosen destination. It's absolutely price driven and those companies appearing at the top of your screen (it's actually called "top screen rate" in the industry) are most likely to get your attention and possibly your business. The volume that can be created by lowest market pricing can deliver cost savings elsewhere in your organisation, which makes that strategy a winning one in terms of margin and profit.

Make it simple

You should be able to describe your USP in one simple sentence. Your customer is very unlikely to remember what it is if it takes a paragraph or short speech to explain exactly what your product or service. If you don't already have it prepared, construct a well-crafted statement which you can produce seamlessly at suitable times to create the interest in your offering which will lead to, at the very least, a positive discussion about the customer owning it.

Service can be a USP

Even if you are selling products, your service can be a USP. For example, if you supply widgets to the engineering sector and the industry norm is a two-week lead-time, if you can deliver within a week you are immediately ahead of your competitors. This will be especially powerful when you are able to translate that benefit in terms which are critical to your customer. The example above would lead to both a reduction in inventory costs as well as increased flexibility to cater for unexpected customer demands. You will be able to convert your USP into real financial benefits therefore, which everyone is interested in.

Remember

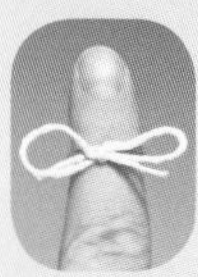

- Really understand your USP.
- Include your USP in your proposition.
- Define it in terms of benefits.
- Make it easy to understand.
- It can be personal to your customer contact.
- Diminish the value of competitors' USPs.
- Use bundling techniques.
- If you sell on price alone make sure you are the lowest.
- Make it simple.

"An objection is not a rejection; it is simply a request for more information."

Bo Bennett

Handling objections

chapter 10

Handling objections

An objection is simply a reason that your prospect or customer gives you not to buy. Sometimes it is a real reason and sometimes it's just an excuse. Now I hate to tell you this but sometimes people will be less than truthful with you. You will remember that I said earlier that in most situations where you are asked to leave literature it's simply because the person concerned isn't brave enough to tell you that they won't buy. So you could say that the literature request is an objection that needs to be handled. Some people will be very upfront with you and simply tell you that they don't want to buy, but beware – you must be certain that it is a real objection before you start to handle it.

Just as an aside, I have very specifically used the word 'handled' rather than 'overcome' objections. The reason for that is simply that I don't believe that you can overcome an objection but maybe that's just me being pedantic. I do think however that you can handle it so that it doesn't prevent you from achieving your objective – an order.

One of the skills that you will need to develop is recognising an objection when the prospect offers it up in your discussion. As I said before, some people will be up front with you and simply say no when you ask for the order but there will be other times during your conversation that a comment is made that is a true objection disguised as a statement – make sure you really listen to what is being said so that you can recognise it and handle it.

Is it real?

We have already acknowledged that it is vital that you establish that the reasons given for not placing an order are real and not just a brush-off. And actually it is probably easier than you might think to do that. You simply have to position the objection as a 'what if'. Once the objection has been stated, your response is something like "If (the objection) didn't exist would you then place an order with me?" If the answer is yes then it really is an objection. Conversely if the answer is no it wasn't a real objection and you start the process again. You ask for the order again and if the response is no then ask why. Again when the objection is given check it's validity by asking the 'what if' question. I would suggest you change your wording with every new objection that is offered but keep checking it to ensure that you don't waste your time trying to handle an objection that doesn't exist.

Handling the real objection

To handle an objection you need benefits and evidence. Once you have established that the reason given really is an issue for your customer you have to find a way to minimise the strength of that objection. Often of course, an objection will be formed through lack of belief or confidence. You may have made a claim during your proposition which is simply unbelievable to the customer. Using evidence from other customers or test and trial results will convince the customer that their fears are unfounded.

“Every sale has five basic obstacles: no need, no money, no hurry, no desire, no trust.”

Zig Ziglar

In their terms

Re-stating the benefits in terms that make sense to your customer will also help to reduce fears or scepticism and at a suitable time it is reasonable for you to ask for the order or commitment again.

The analogy which may explain this whole issue in very clear terms is imagining that you have an A4 sheet of paper with the word 'objection' in front of you. Well actually, let's put it in front of your customer so that the word is 3 or 4 inches away from his or her face. In that position the person concerned cannot see past that sheet of paper and the word 'objection' because it is the only thing within the line of vision. And that's why you are not about to get an order because that objection is so big and the buyer is blinkered. Your role is to gradually move that piece of paper, and the offending word, away from the customer's face so that it becomes less and less significant. The evidence and reiteration of benefits will make the paper move until it is the size of a postage stamp and so far away that the word is illegible! Now take your order.

Phrasing benefits

Knowing the benefits that you, your product or service, or your company can offer is just the starting point. To handle objections effectively you need to be able to present them in such a way that the recipient of the benefit really does get enough value that the proposition becomes irresistible. Given that these objections are often centred on a lack of belief and/or confidence you need to present some evidence which will allay those fears. I mentioned tests and trials previously and these really can come into play in this situation. You might like to practise using some of the following phrases to help handle the objections that have been put in the way of your next order:

"In tests that we have carried out in our laboratory, we have found that typically, in applications exactly the same as yours, our product lasts twice as long as the product that you currently use."

"You probably know of (name of another company in the same sector) and they have found that by switching the service provision to us they have improved their productivity by 35%."

"If you'd like to look at this results analysis you will see that against all of our major competitors we come out top in terms of performance and value."

Obviously you will want to tailor these not only to your own offering but to your own style. You need to be happy and confident making these statements and you will only be able to do that by doing so in a manner which suits.

Confidence breeds confidence

At no time in the sales process is appearing confident more important that now. Confidence is contagious! The real benefit of that is simple; if you appear totally confident in your response to the objection given, the benefit statement will carry so much more weight and you are likely to be believed. You only have to consider the way the stock market fluctuates often based on confidence—or lack of it—in one particular sector or product. Oil prices often rise because there is a 'fear' that a crisis or conflict in the oil-producing region will reduce supply. Before anything actually happens to restrict that supply, the prices start to rise simply through a lack of confidence.

Some people just seem to have that air of confidence, and if you don't you have to ensure that you find a way of at least appearing as if you do. Often simply having total knowledge about your subject and the benefits will give you that confidence. It's also useful to have that library of testimonials and test results with you at all times so you can refer to them and deliver the confident statement which will make the difference between success and failure.

Remember

- Check that objections are real before handling them.
- Use appropriate questioning techniques to confirm.
- Get out early so that you can handle and proceed.
- Use evidence and testimonials.
- Be confident in your statements and products.
- Phrase benefits to suit the specific company or individual.

"Until the deal closes, each company will continue to operate independently, and it is business as usual."

Tom Siebel

Closing the sale

chapter 11
Closing the sale

As crazy as it may seem, the part of the sales call that many sales people seem to dread the most is asking for the order. That's what you are there for after all but it can be a nervy situation – especially for someone new to sales. I think the reason that this part is so difficult for some people is simply the fear that the buyer will say no – a rejection. If that's the case you just need to check why (**Handling objections section**) and do a little more restating of your benefits.

There are many different ways of closing and most of them are not at all frightening. This is simply another part of the sales process which both parties know will happen at some point and therefore shouldn't be avoided.

If you think back to the section about the idea of salesmen having the gift of the gab it usually creates a perception of a high pressure closer who puts a huge amount of effort into making the customer buy. It really doesn't have to be like that and you can take a very gentle approach, and before you know where you are you will be tying up the loose ends of this first order. Remember that no is simply a response to a question – just the same as yes is! So look for the buying signals—a statement, question or gesture that demonstrates interest—and ask if you can proceed with the order.

This is almost always perceived as the most difficult part of the sales call – but it really doesn't have to be.

Go on – just ask!

Some trainers will tell you to start closing as soon as you start talking. They fondly describe it as ABC – Always Be Closing. I don't agree. I believe that what is likely to happen is that your customer will feel pushed into doing something they may not want to do or are not yet ready to do. But don't worry – there are some simple techniques you can use which really don't feel like pressurising your customer at all. A big favourite and one of the easiest is simply to offer an alternative:

"Which day is best for you to receive delivery – Tuesday or Friday?"

"Which distributor would you prefer to supply you, Smith's or Brown's?"

"We pack these in boxes of 24 or 48; which would be best for you?"

You are simply asking a question – and the answer is your order. This may lead you into some form of negotiation but that's OK; if the customer is about to give you some commitment to buy then negotiation is the right thing to happen at this stage.

Referred close

This is a simple technique that relies on the buyer's knowledge of his market and the other players within it. By implying that a competitor of the prospect company is gaining significant benefits from buying your product they will feel compelled to react. By imply I don't mean to suggest something that is untrue; I simply mean that confidentiality dictates that you cannot divulge details of transactions between yourself and other parties. What you can do however, is explain that "Other companies in your sector have found that by switching to our products (or service) they have managed to increase productivity by up to 27%". The benefit that you state can be any that your proposition gives but financial benefits are almost always the strongest. Use cost savings, waste reduction, quality improvements, gaining market share and any others that are relevant and significant in your prospect's market sector.

You can make this type of close even stronger if you can gain permission from your existing customers to use their name as a testimonial. Then you really can put the pressure on to buy by explaining that a competitor of theirs "has a more productive manufacturing process as a result of using my product".

Empathy close

Assuming that you have blueprinted properly in the early part of the sale you will have a clear understanding of the issues that are important to your customer – either the company or the individual. Therefore by taking one or more of those issues and wrapping it up in a 'close' you can ensure that the benefits of doing business with you are clear.

Let's take an example of a retail outlet that currently buys from the largest supply company in the market. The situation is that, because the supplier is the largest, they have to use the largest vehicles to deliver such large volumes of stock to their broad customer base. This causes inconvenience because these large vehicles cannot get down the narrow service road behind the retail premises and therefore stop on the restricted parking area at the front of the shop. As a consequence the driver walks through the showroom with boxes of product. This not only disrupts traffic flow immediately outside your premises but is an unwanted disturbance to your browsing customers as the driver walks through the showroom, bumping his or her way past shelves and display stands with your delivery.

Because your delivery vehicles are smaller they can access the rear of the premises, preventing the difficulties described above. Your close therefore is "Because we understand the needs of our customers to make discreet deliveries which do not affect the normal trading conditions that they have, we have designed our logistics around the use of smaller delivery vehicles and efficient delivery schedules. Would that suit you better and enable you to carry on serving your own customers without disruption?" Surely the answer has to be "Yes"?

Your personal close

The most important part of every element of the sales process is to appear relaxed and confident. Having that air of confidence is perhaps even more important in this area of closing the sale. So why not make up your own closing techniques? Think about what type of conversation suits your style the most. What style do you feel most comfortable with? And in a specific customer, what style or approach do you think that the buyer will react most positively to? Have the same attitude to the close as you have to the questioning techniques and seeing it as no more than a continuation of the previous conversation you've been having. Remember that people like to buy rather than be sold to, so your question about closing the deal is no more than you offering your buyer some help to make his buying decision.

What's best for both?

Negotiation is not the same as selling... but most sales situations will, at some point, involve at least some negotiation. Learning to become a successful negotiator will help you be successful in everything that you do – both at work and at home. A successful negotiation will leave both parties feeling happy with the outcome. Obviously therefore, it is not going to be how much you can get out of your customer but more about what situation would leave both of you pleased with the prospect of doing business together. Remember that you are in this for the long-term relationship – not a quick hit never to be repeated. I'll cover negotiation at some length in the next chapter because it is such a vital part of the process and can be the factor in determining how valuable the deal is.

The price is right – well it should be

Price is potentially a sticking point for many deals. The customer always wants the lowest price – and you always want the highest. Before you start talking price make sure you have as much information about the CURRENT costs as possible. And actually, don't talk 'price', talk 'cost'... there is a big difference. If your product costs twice as much as your customer but lasts four times as long it's actually half the 'cost'. You can't assume your customer will make that connection, so you must – it's the very best way to strike a deal.

What happens if you don't close?

The simple answer is that the customer is unlikely to buy. There will be occasions where the customer will ask if he or she can buy from you despite your reluctance to show that you want to have their business. However, you can't rely on that happening and you take a large risk that your trading relationship will stall before it has started if you are not prepared to make that close.

Remember

- Look for the best opportunities to "close".
- Use the information you have gained to form the "close".
- Use a variety of techniques.
- Be relaxed.
- Use a conversational style.
- Be brave – don't be afraid of rejection.
- Talk about "cost" not "price".
- Just ask!

“The single most powerful tool for winning a negotiation is the ability to get up and walk away from the table without a deal.”

Anon

Negotiating techniques

chapter 12

Negotiating techniques

Negotiation	–	"To talk with others in order to reach an agreement".
Selling	–	"To exchange for money".

What is it?

Negotiation is the process of searching for an agreement that satisfies both parties. A real negotiation implies a win-win situation, in which all parties are satisfied.

Why use it?

To avoid dominance by one or more parties and to ensure a win-win situation where both parties get their needs met.

Negotiation versus selling

There is certainly confusion about whether negotiation and sales are the same. Let me put that to bed right now – the truth is they are not. You could put it simply by saying that sales is the process that allows the customer to buy something the supplier wants to sell. Negotiation is the discussion around the terms under which that transaction takes place; the detail, most of which will be commercial. Most sales people are trained in Selling Skills but surprisingly, most are not given Negotiation Skills training. For some reason many companies leave that subject matter for senior managers.

This situation not only surprises but alarms me because good negotiation techniques are a critical part of the process and can easily add 10% to sales revenues, and this goes straight to the bottom line as profit because it attracts no additional sales (or other) cost. I'm going to spend more time on this topic than I have on some of the others simply because I feel that it is so important and yet so few sales professionals have developed the edge in the negotiation element of agreeing a sale.

When to negotiate

Sales negotiation is an increasingly important part of the sales process. Negotiation starts when buyer and seller are conditionally committed to the sale (do not be drawn into negotiation before the principles of a sale agreement have been reached) the buyer is very likely to attempt to bring the negotiation into play before the sale has been agreed.
As I said before, the negotiation element of the sales process will have a fundamental affect on the attractiveness of the deal and is therefore vital to the financial results of the selling organisation.

Negotiation generally results in a price compromise between seller and buyer but don't restrict it to that element of the agreement – there are many other conditions which can be negotiated and will influence the attractiveness of the outcome. Therefore under no circumstances whatsoever start the negotiation process before you have that agreement to do business.

If in doubt............ask another question.

If you are not sure that the customer is conditionally committed to the sale, then ask a conditional closing question, i.e. "If we can agree the details will you go ahead?" If the answer is "No" you still have some selling to do. Once ground has been conceded it cannot be regained and you immediately give the position of strength to the other person.

Which approach?

These days, the aim of negotiation should focus on collaboration rather than traditional confrontation, or a winner-takes-all result. Although the temptation of most sales people is to create a winning result, for the long-term benefit of the business relationship the collaborative approach will yield the best overall results. The ideal method is to think creatively and work in co-operation with the other side.

Partnership approach

By developing a **partnership** approach during the negotiation you are already building trust and confidence in your business relationship. It should go without saying that, unless you are the double glazing salesman that I spoke of in the opening pages, you are looking to build that long-term relationship with your new found customer, so approaching this critical part of the sales process in the right way is vital.

A partnership approach entails both parties outlining the issues or conditions that are important to them and doing everything they can to reach agreement where each side achieves as many of those conditions as possible.

From a sales perspective, once you have found out which issues are potential deal breakers for your customer, you have to do everything feasible to satisfy them. The issues which are less important are much more likely to be conceded by each party. If all goes well, the critical issues for your customer will not be critical for you, so let the customer have them. In turn you can then take a more rigid stance for critical issues for your own organisation.

What are the needs of each party?

As a starting point it's a very good idea to write a list of the issues that are important to each side. Remember to include personal and emotional elements because these are just as important as commercial issues. The contents of that list represent a 'cost' to each party, either to give or concede, and the individual costs will vary.

As part of your negotiation evaluate the costs from your perspective to help you determine which are more important than others. Remember that negotiations are often about finding that middle ground between two starting points, by offering one or more concessions from the customer's list you can ask for some from your list to be agreed.

Who goes first?

Whoever makes the opening offer is undoubtedly at a disadvantage. If you go first, the buyer can choose to disregard it and ask for a better offer. And the buyer avoids the risk of making an offer themselves that is more beneficial than you would have been prepared to accept. It's amazing how often a buyer is prepared to pay more than an asking price, but avoids

“Cash can buy,
but it takes
enthusiasm to sell.”

Anon

having to do so because they keep quiet and let the seller go first. The reverse is obviously also true. The key therefore is to let the other side go first. Sometimes you will be pleasantly surprised at what the buyer expects to pay, which obviously enables you to adjust your aim. Letting the other side go first is a simple and effective tactic that is often overlooked.

Opportunity to walk

Letting the buyer go first on price or cost also enables you to use another tactic, whereby you refuse to even accept the invitation to start negotiating, which you should do if the price or cost point is completely unacceptable or a 'silly offer'. This then forces the other side to go again or at least re-think their expectations or stance, which can amount to a huge movement in your favour, before you have even started.

Success is influenced by pressure

In your selling position, if you have lots of other potential customers, and therefore can walk away without fear of failure in your overall achievement of targets, the pressure is off you and the relaxed approach that you can adopt is likely to bring you success. If you are desperate for this sale you are clearly much more likely to concede early and lose any advantage that you may otherwise have been able to negotiate – that additional 10% revenue and profit.

The same will apply to your customer of course, and that's exactly why many buyers will give you the impression that they can go somewhere else – even if they can't or don't want to. They know that this weak position gives you the advantage.

Call my bluff

This therefore means that when you are in the sales position, the more you can create the impression that there is no alternative comparable supplier, the stronger your position. You have to create the perception that your product or service is unique, and that the other person has nowhere else to go; he cannot afford to walk away. This positioning of uniqueness is the most important tactic, and it comes into play before you even start to negotiate. If your product offer is not unique remember that you are part of it.

You can still create a unique position by the way that you conduct yourself; build trust, rapport, and empathy with the other person. Establishing a position (or impression) of uniqueness is the single most effective technique when you are selling, whereas denying uniqueness is the most powerful tactic of the buyer.

Aim for the stars!

Aim for your best outcome – a good buyer will always aim low and given that they will always ask you to start the negotiating process, if you aim too low you've lost ground immediately. Remember that your very first offer represents the absolute best outcome that you can achieve. It will never get better and almost always get worse. Conversely, that opening positioning of yours represents the minimum expectation of the customer.

The psychology of negotiation

More often than not negotiations come down to little more than finding the centre ground between two starting points. The thing you must try to find is the other person's 'break point'. Everyone has one and once you know where that is you can aim for your best outcome. It's also worth remembering that the easier the negotiation the less satisfying it is.

Take for example, your attempts to buy a house. The sale price is £250,000 and after viewing you put in an offer for £200,000 which is immediately accepted. How do you feel? I would guess that your immediate reaction is delight because you have managed to get what you want at a real knock down price. Then you sleep on it and wake up the next day feeling that the vendor dropped such a large amount of money so quickly that, actually, they would have dropped more or you have bought a pup!

Alternatively, if your offer of £200,000 was refused and the vendor asked you to move nearer to the asking price and suggested £230,000, you might end up settling at £220,000. You have therefore paid 10% (£20,000) more than in the first scenario but psychologically, you are likely to feel more satisfied with the outcome. The same emotions will be present with your sales negotiation.

Political pressures

Don't forget that your customer will have political issues to handle too. The quality of the outcome from his perspective may have a significant influence on his own position within his organisation. Several successful contract negotiations might be the key to promotion or salary increases. That buyer might have more to gain or lose than just what happens in your specific negotiation. Once again, if you are aware of that you can help in giving the right concessions to maximise his needs while minimising the cost to you.

Give and take

Never give away a concession without getting something in return. Depending on the approach taken by the customer they may not want to offer anything at all. If that is the case you are not in negotiation. You are simply in a situation where something has been offered to you at a very specific set of conditions and all you have to do is decide whether you want to accept it or not. This is not an unusual stance for buyers to take and I would urge you to resist if those demands are too high. Walk away and find a more reasonable (and profitable) customer.

If you start your trading relationship that way, no matter how long your do business together, that dynamic will always exist – give on your part and take on the customer's. The only time it might stop is if there is a change of personnel.

Remember the big picture

A tactic often used by buyers is to attempt to break up the conditions of doing business into small chunks and gain an advantage in each one. The chances are that, because they are smaller pieces, you might concede more easily because you are thinking of the end result. Or at least you are thinking of the end result as it stood when this process started, but by the time you reach it you will realise that you have agreed to something that is different from what you thought. So that's why you need to keep the big picture in your mind at all times.

Note keeping

Make sure that you keep detailed notes as the negotiation proceeds. You won't remember everything a day or two later so it's vital to do it as you go. It also prevents either party from 'remembering it differently' further down the line. Because you will be making these as you go you can also demonstrate that you are interpreting what has been agreed correctly by summarising what you have written. Also make sure that you give the customer a copy of those notes – both photocopied handwritten notes on the day and a follow-up of typed records of the discussion soon afterwards. (The sooner the better while everything is still fresh in both party's minds.)

Calling a halt to negotiations

If the break point that your customer is adopting is just too demanding or not commercially viable, you must kill it there and then. Just come right out and say it – "I just can't get to that position. If that is what it's going to take for us to trade then I'm sorry to say I'll have to walk away."

Of course this might (and sometimes definitely will) lead to a breakdown and no business being conducted but it might also bring about a shift in position of your customer. It really does depend on that pressure position – how much each of you wants to do business with the other. Don't sell your soul – you will always regret it. Be brave enough to walk away.

Celebrate the deal

Once the deal has been struck make sure you celebrate in some way. That might be as simple as shaking hands and smiling – or it could mean a bottle of champagne over dinner. You can decide what the most appropriate method is yourself as long as you do something. This is the start of what you hope will be a long-standing trading relationship so why not get it off to a great start? It may well also differentiate you from your competitors as many sales people do not behave in that way. Create the impression to your customer that this is an important milestone in working together and that you are truly entering into a "partnership" rather than just a customer/supplier relationship.

Record the agreement

It is very important after you have concluded your negotiation to confirm the details in writing. This gives you the opportunity to set out all the details of the products or services as well as any Service Level Agreement if relevant. It prevents ambiguity later in the relationship and should include prices, settlement, and terms and conditions of business.

Remember

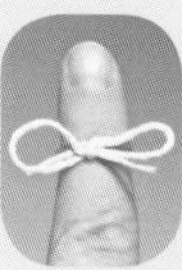

- Don't start too early.
- Never go first!
- Use a collaborative approach.
- Create a unique position.
- Plan your position in advance.
- Put a 'cost' on the critical issues for both parties.
- This is not a Dutch auction - unless you make it so.
- Aim high.
- Be prepared to walk away.
- Celebrate the deal.
- Confirm in writing.

I am the world's worst salesman, therefore, I must make it easy for people to buy.

F.W. Wooloworth

Key Account Management – a brief introduction

chapter 13

Key Account Management

- a brief introduction

The most surprising thing about Key Account Management is that so few companies adopt it as their default way of working. It is my view that this approach should absolutely dominate the way every company thinks and plans its activity. It is so much more than a sales strategy – it's a company strategy. It should dictate almost every element of how a company operates, and all decisions should refer back to the Key Account Management Plan. If the actions support the Key Account Management Plan then go ahead; if they don't then why are you doing it?

Most elements of Key Account Management are fundamental and easily identified. It's mostly common sense and structure. It's hugely effective if carried out correctly which is why it should be used by more companies.

You need your company to behave in a way that supports rather than hinders you; it really is true to say that some organisations operate in such a way that selling becomes very difficult.

This is such a huge subject in itself that I am only going to touch on it here. It warrants an entire book so I merely want to give you an understanding of the principles so that you can explore them yourself and consider adopting this method to grow your customer base and the yield from it.

A definition

Key Account Management (KAM) is simply a way of operating so that you build strong, sustainable and mutually rewarding relationships by working in a collaborative way, focussing every element of what you do on its relevance to that relationship. In its purest sense your organisation will develop its Business Plan in support of KAM and indeed the organisational structure will be created to ensure the right people are in the right roles doing the right things to optimise the supplier/customer relationship.

How many accounts?

Considered wisdom suggests that any organisation can only handle around 35 Key Accounts. The outer limits are 5-50 but somewhere in between would be more appropriate. That means that you as an individual are likely to have no more than 2 or 3 Key Accounts.

The reason is simple: to give the focus and attention of your entire organisation, which your Key Account customer needs to enable them to grow disproportionately, that focus and attention needs to be concentrated. You can't do that with too many accounts.

There is plenty of evidence of organisations that have run a hugely successful Key Account Management programme with 30 accounts and doubled that number with the belief that they will then be even more successful. The reality is that the original list starts to fail due to the lack of focus, resource and attention. They become 'ordinary' merely by their number.

Knowledge is the key

It's absolutely impossible to create a strategic plan for your customers if you don't know enough about them.

And of course, if you don't know enough about your partner customers how can you empathise with them? I have included a number of forms at the end of this chapter (p146-p152) to help you identify the issues that you need to have knowledge of in order to adopt a KAM programme. By completing these information-gathering forms you will put yourself, and therefore your company, in a position to satisfy the needs of the customer and grow a strong relationship with them. Because it is a partnership approach you can only do this with a customer who wants to be your partner.

It can't be forced and you may have to sell the benefits of the relationship as it will mean each company sharing, sometimes sensitive, information with each other. So trust and integrity is vital – one break in that trust and the whole relationship can fail.

Strength in contact

In any business relationship the strength is determined not only by the quality of relationship, but quantity too. The more people from each organisation who know, communicate and trust each other, the stronger that relationship is and the more difficult it is to break (by a competitor). The analogy that I like to use is simple: the strength gained in fixing two objects together is dependent on their shape.

If you join two triangles together with glue at the point, that joining will be weak:

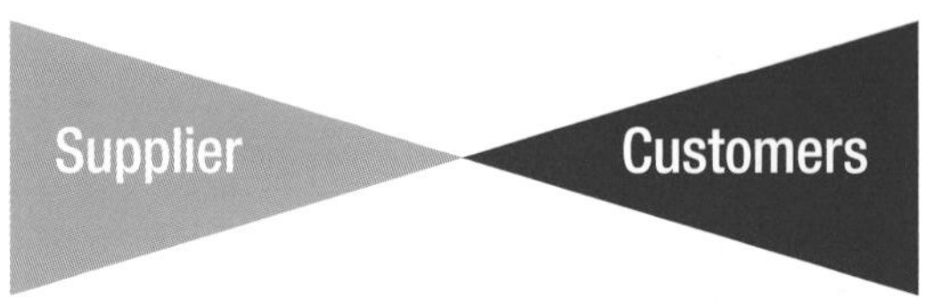

If however, you join them at their bases, that joining will be much stronger:

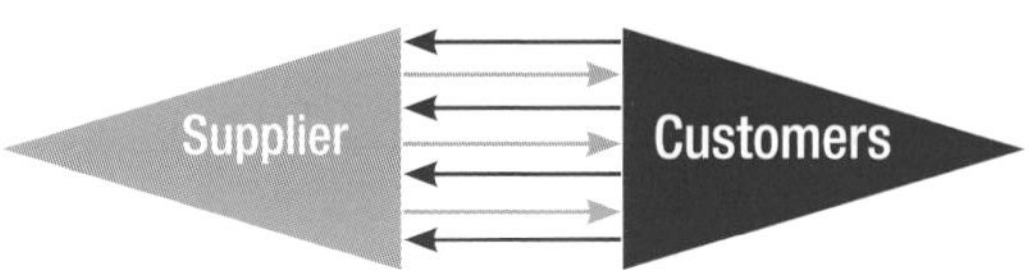

The key is therefore to have as many relevant points of contact as possible to secure the 'join'. Relevant does of course mean the right people in your organisation communicating with the right people in the customer organisation:

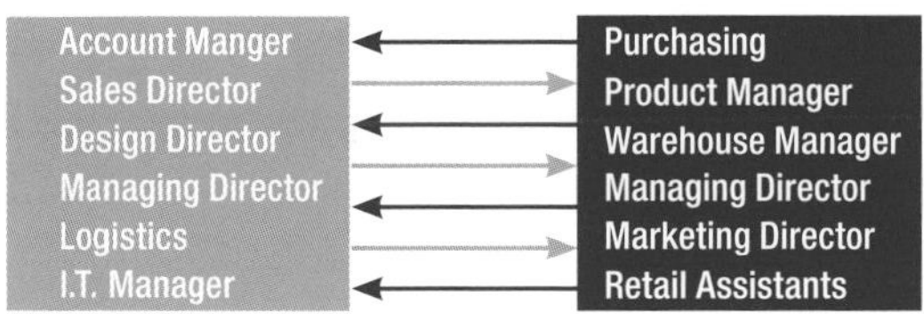

"In sales, a referral is the key to the door of resistance."

Bo Bennett

A partnership

KAM is fundamentally about a partnership approach. It entails giving and receiving sometimes sensitive information and including the other party in decision making which will affect the relationship.

If one side tries to win against the other it won't work – both sides must want mutual prosperity, and respect the need for profit generation and productivity improvements. Take a look at the forms that follow which will give you the framework for starting a KAM approach and if you are not already using this approach, why not find a suitable book to take you through the steps and methods of sustaining a strong, rewarding and enjoyable trading relationship?

Hold regular reviews

An important part of the whole Key Account Management process is to regularly review your activity formally. By definition, many people from each party will be involved in the whole process and these reviews are an excellent communication vehicle to ensure all relevant people are updated on activity. Record minutes of these reviews and circulate not only to the "members" of the KAM team but also other interested parties within each organisation.

Plan for the future

As Key Account Management is a very strategic approach to customer relationship management it will inherently contain medium and long term planning. By exploring the future goals and plans of each organisation, connections and synergies can be identified and built upon. You may also gain subsidiary benefits by understanding projected market trends, which you may be able to capitalise on with other customers within the sector. Your own company's product development can also benefit by this industry knowledge and identification of future opportunities.

Remember

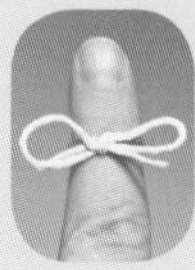

- Can only use with 2 or 3 customers.
- Needs total company support.
- A partnership approach.
- Create a broad contact surface to ensure a strong bond.
- Use a structured approach.
- Drive all activity through your KAM plan.
- Review your activity regularly.
- Make necessary changes along the way.
- Review regularly.
- Plan for the future.

Useful forms

How well do you know your Key Account?

Score each element out of 10:

0 = not at all 10 = couldn't be better

Do you know...	Score
Your key customer's products and how you add value to them?	
The customer's strategic plan?	
The customer's financial health (ratios etc.)?	
The customer's business processes (logistics, purchasing, production etc.)?	
What the customer values/needs from its suppliers?	
Your proportion of the customer's spending?	
Which of your competitors the customer uses; why and how it rates them?	
How much attributable (interface) costs should be allocated to your customer?	
The real profitability of the customer to you?	
How long it takes to make a profit on a major new customer?	
Total	

Score as a percentage %

That's how much you know about your KEY customer...

Relationships

Account Manager: Customer:

What type of relationship do you want – how would you describe it?

What type of relationship does your customer want?

How close are you to (1) above (%)? ....

How close are you to (2) above (%)? ....

What do you need to do to achieve (1)?

What do you need to do to achieve (2)?

Segmentation

Customer: ___________________________________

Consider the key issues for this customer resulting from the SWOT analysis.

Critical Success Factors

Critical Success Factor	Action plan

Relationship contact surface

Account Manager: Customer:

Supplier		Customer	
Name	Position	Name	Position

Checklist

Score: 0 = not at all   10 = couldn't be better

	Have you...	Score
1	Categorised your customers?	
2	Matched your relationship with each customer type?	
3	An up-to-date copy of your customer's organisational chart?	
4	Got a good understanding of the relevance and authority of each contact?	
5	Got an understanding about how each contact views your company?	
6	Looked at the overall picture and identified relationship gaps?	
7	Got strong relationships with key decision makers?	
8	Support from colleagues in the relevant functions to be part of the overall relationship with your customer?	
9	Got all levels in the customer covered?	
10	The ability and opportunity to solve glitches in the process?	
11	Helped improve your customer's margin?	
12	Become a good source of information for your customer regarding issues that are not easily available, i.e. market trends, research data etc.?	
13	Offered them expert advice on something new or difficult?	
14	Delivered training to their staff to help them market/use your products more effectively?	
	Total	

Score ....../140   As a percentage   %

You have now identified which areas of your Key Account Management you need to work on.

Key Account Management

Account Manager: ______________________________

Sector: ______________________________

What major activities will you become involved in to ensure you adopt a Key Account Management approach?

Activity	Target date
1	
2	
3	
4	
5	
6	
7	
8	
9	
10	

How committed are you to make these activities happen? Circle one number...

1 2 3 4 5 6 7 8 9 10

In the end...

As I said at the beginning of this book, my aim is to give you straightforward and clear advice on how to improve your effectiveness and therefore success in your sales career. It can be a very rewarding career, giving you the opportunity to meet hundreds of people and learn about many industries.

By having a well thought out and structured approach I'm sure that you'll be successful. Make sure that everything you do is a conscious decision with a clear objective at the end of it. And don't forget how important those elements of communication are; after all, you are in the communications business.

In order to create confidence in your product, service and company, you must plan well, maintain control and be self-assured in your approach. The success that you enjoy will be directly linked not only to the effort that you are prepared to put in but also the attitude that you adopt. Remember Cliff Young, who proved that almost anything is possible if you have the right attitude to your task.

Remember to practise all the things that you need to be good at. See your sales career in the same way as a athlete or actor sees their own career; the more practice or rehearsal you put in the better you are likely to be.

Work hard, be successful and enjoy many years of rewarding negotiations and profitable closures.

Happy Selling!

“The best salesman ever was the one who sold two milking machines to a farmer who had only one cow. The salesman helped finance the deal by taking the cow as a down payment on the two milking machines.”

Herbert V. Prochnow

Recommended Reading

Body Language – Instant Manager
by Dick Thompson and Geoff Ribbens

Communicating – using NLP to Supercharge your Business Skills
by Ian R McLaren

C.R.M Pocketbook
by David Alexander & Charles Turner

Excel 2007 for Dummies
by Greg Harvey

The Greatest Marketing Tips in the World
by Catriona MacKay

The Greatest Personal Success Tips in the World
by Brian Larcher

Life's a Pitch
by Stephen Bayley & Roger Mavity

The Revolution in Sales and Marketing
by Allan J Magrath

Tricks of the Mind
by Derren Brown

Your notes

Index

'The Greatest Tips in the World' books

Baby & Toddler Tips
ISBN 978-1-905151-70-7

Barbeque Tips
ISBN 978-1-905151-68-4

Breastfeeding Tips
ISBN 978-1-905151-34-0

Cat Tips
ISBN 978-1-905151-66-0

Collecting Tips
ISBN 978-1-905151-42-4

Cookery Tips
ISBN 978-1-905151-64-6

Cricketing Tips
ISBN 978-1-905151-18-9

DIY Tips
ISBN 978-1-905151-62-2

Dog Tips
ISBN 978-1-905151-67-7

Etiquette & Dining Tips
ISBN 978-1-905151-21-9

Fishing Tips
ISBN 978-1-905151-32-2

Freelance Writing Tips
ISBN 978-1-905151-17-2

Gardening Tips
ISBN 978-1-905151-60-8

Genealogy Tips
ISBN 978-1-905151-72-1

Golfing Tips
ISBN 978-1-905151-63-9

Horse & Pony Tips
ISBN 978-1-905151-19-6

Household Tips
ISBN 978-1-905151-61-5

Life Coaching Tips
ISBN 978-1-905151-23-3

Management Tips
ISBN 978-1-905151-44-8

Marketing Tips
ISBN 978-1-905151-41-7

Moving Abroad Tips
ISBN 978-1-905151-47-9

Personal Success Tips
ISBN 978-1-905151-71-4

Photography Tips
ISBN 978-1-905151-39-4

Podcasting Tips
ISBN 978-1-905151-75-2

Property Developing Tips
ISBN 978-1-905151-69-1

Relationship & Dating Tips
ISBN 978-1-905151-35-6

Retirement Tips
ISBN 978-1-905151-28-8

Sales Tips
ISBN 978-1-905151-40-0

Sex Tips
ISBN 978-1-905151-74-5

Slimming & Healthy Living Tips
ISBN 978-1-905151-31-8

Tax Tips
ISBN 978-1-905151-43-1

Travel Tips
ISBN 978-1-905151-73-8

Wedding Tips
ISBN 978-1-905151-27-1

Pet Recipe books

The Greatest Feline Feasts in the World
ISBN 978-1-905151-50-9

The Greatest Doggie Dinners in the World
ISBN 978-1-905151-51-6

'The Greatest in the World' DVDs

The Greatest in the World – Gardening Tips

The Greatest in the World – Yoga Tips

The Greatest in the World – Cat & Kitten Tips

The Greatest in the World – Dog & Puppy Tips

For more information about currently available and forthcoming book and DVD titles please visit:

www.the**greatest**inthe**world**.com

or write to:

The Greatest in the World Ltd
PO Box 3182
Stratford-upon-Avon
Warwickshire CV37 7XW
United Kingdom

Tel / Fax: +44(0)1789 299616
Email: info@thegreatestintheworld.com

The author

Gary Collins is a Sales Coach and Management Trainer. Having spent most of his sales career in Sales Management he recently started his own company to pursue his passion of Sales Improvement. After an initial spell working with his father, Gary commenced his very successful career with 3M Company, the global blue chip noted for innovation and creativity. Having started as a territory sales representative Gary's career developed at regular intervals culminating with a European Business Development role.

Gary now operates across many sectors and markets, coaching both individuals and groups to achieve improved techniques and therefore organisational financial results.